C000008445

The Won(

The Black Sea

By the Same Author

The Wonders of Nepal

The Wonders of The Black Sea

Tales of A Grandmother – Volume 2

Audrey Forsyth

Distribution in the United Kingdom and worldwide by Ingram Spark

A CIP catalogue record is available from the British library

Cover/Page Designs by Graham Forsyth and indieauthorsworld.com

Front Cover Illustration : - Audrey discovered some beautiful arts
and crafts in Lima, Peru and brought home this decorated paper
mâché, double door, front opening, container within which was
hidden, also in finely worked paper mâché, a musical instrument
shop complete with a large number of all types of instruments.

Photographs: Graham Forsyth

Maps: Graham Forsyth

The publishers and authors have done their best to ensure the
accuracy of all the information in this publication, however they
cannot accept any responsibility for any loss, injury or inconvenience
sustained by any traveller as a result of information or advice
contained in this.

Published with the help of Indie Authors World
indieauthorsworld.com

IndieAuthors
World

One Day at A Time

A Personal Divertimento
On

The Wonders of
the Black Sea

Istanbul, Trabzon (Turkey)
Sochi (Russia)
Yalta, Sevastopol, Odessa (Ukraine)
Constanza(Romania)
Nessebur (Bulgaria)

2nd - 13th October 2008

*"The real voyage of discovery consists not in seeking new landscapes
but in having new eyes"* - **Marcel Proust**.

The Caucasus (1829) - Alexander Pushkin

"Below me the silver-capped Caucasus lies ….
Nearby an abyss yawns, and, far down , a roaring
Stream swift rushes past; o'er the peaks calmly soaring,
An eagle seems motionless, pinned to the skies.
Here rivers are born that mid rocks, grumbling, wander
And landslides begin with a crash of thunder."

"All the books in this little series are the produce of
my travels and are dedicated, with my love, to
each of my wonderful grandchildren, both
born and unborn, who enlighten my
every day. My earnest wish is that
these notes and photographs
may encourage them a little
during their lives to grow
to love language,
travel, culture,
history and
people as
I have."

Audrey Forsyth

September 2013

Reviews

After reading this book my first thoughts were what energy and enthusiasm on the part of Audrey. For her to encompass all the sightseeing and socializing in twelve days is an unbelievable accomplishment.

Audrey's accounts are peppered with countless interesting stories including those relating to the poet Pushkin, the Ukrainian Tolstoy family, Beautiful Odessa, Tsar Nicholas ll, Sevastopol and the Crimean War, Stalin's Green Dacha, Chekhov's White House, Liszt's Piano and even Dracula.

The Black Sea, I found out, is a place also steeped in history with each country having its own version of myths and legend.

The large number of photographs accompanying Audrey's journey are equally enlightening and bring to life the richness of the interiors of the buildings and places visited.

I really felt I was on the journey too. A wonderful experience.

This book really is a must for anyone visiting or interested in the Black Sea area.

Janette Smith

I found much to whet a wish to visit this region which means it is a good travel book.

There are marvellous descriptions and pictures e.g. Sumela Monastery, Stalin's dacha and the Vorontsov palace.

Audrey's knowledge of Russia and its language also helped the atmosphere eg seeing Chekhov's nameplate on his door.

This book would appeal to the armchair traveller or to anyone contemplating a Visit to the Black Sea.

Audrey's warm personality, intelligence and humour permeate the descriptions and give them veracity. This would make someone want to follow in her footsteps. It would certainly tempt me towards any other books in the series.

It is a fascinating picture of this pivotal area touched — in history, and still today — by so many people and events.

Rosemary Combe

Contents

Series Preface

The writer of this book, Audrey, had a reserved personality, a wicked sense of humour, an astonishing intellect and a lifetime spent working as a regular primary school teacher.

So what made her produce over 10 separate comprehensive travel experience stories, unpublished in her lifetime?

This may help to explain…

Audrey Ferrier Munro Forsyth, nee Smith, was born in 1946 and brought up in the small Angus village of Kirriemuir in Scotland, which is best known as the birthplace of J. M. Barrie who wrote Peter Pan.

Their family farm inheritance had been previously siphoned off through lawyer embezzlement, before being passed on to them.

An only child her great joy was music, of which she excelled at sight reading, playing various instruments but primarily the piano in which she achieved high grades.

In 1964 she trained as a primary teacher in Dundee and it was there she met, Graham, studying civil engineering, who became her husband of 44 years and whose work would take them and family around the country.

They were married in Edinburgh in 1969 their two boys being born in the 70s.

Her teaching life included the extremes of working with children in deprived areas, whom she enjoyed being with, as well as a position of deputy headship in a girls preparatory school.

Though not a professionally trained musician her musical abilities were always fully utilised and loved by the school children whether for hymns at assembly, the musical accompaniment to all the school productions or songs in the classroom.

Her greatest relaxation was playing piano transcriptions of the music of the great composers, often operas , straight through for an hour or so.

A polyglot throughout her life she had French, Italian and Spanish as her European language base and in her final years she became highly conversant in Russian, too.

Travel was her addiction, music her passion and family her love.

Being a voracious reader, embroiderer, crossword fanatic and travel anecdote raconteur were only a few of her other interests and activities.

Ill health, however, affected her off and on throughout her married life, resulting in early retirement from teaching.

In hindsight it is likely her then symptoms along with existing health problems obscured her underlying pancreatic cancer condition which was diagnosed in 2012 and took her life in 2013.

She and Graham had done much travelling, despite her poor health, it being an opportunity for her to use her languages to full effect and enjoy the history and people of the countries visited, always scribing copious notes on all she saw and experienced.

Her terminal condition brought about a great need and urgent desire for her to put these notes into the form of a journal which she then wanted to be completed in book form for grandchildren to read as teenagers.

At this stage they had six grandchildren and two on the way. The completion of these manuscripts, 10 in all, and at some cost, she achieved.

So was born ' *Tales of a Grandmother* ' in which all her lifelong interests in music, geography, history, language, travel and people are so deeply immersed and so eloquently and often humorously expressed.

Drafts of some of these were read and enjoyed by the nursing staff who latterly provided her medical care showing it was clear that these were of interest to a greater audience than just her grandchildren.

She would have wanted the reader to enjoy them too.

---oOo---

Introduction

In the preface I outlined briefly my late wife's biography and the circumstances which had brought about her research, preparation and completion of her Travelogue manuscripts.

This included the final drafts of a number of books - over 10 in all - which Audrey had hand written then dictated in order to quickly achieve a completed text.

I had supported her throughout this time both computer-wise, and proof reading in order to help her to achieve her goal. The photo below shows her hard at work in our Perthshire garden.

Naturally her expressed wish was for me subsequently to complete these in book form with the inclusion of many of the photographs I had taken at the time of our travels, in order to illustrate her texts.

With the inclusion of some additional illustrations this I have done and I have endeavoured to achieve the object of her desires.

Graham Forsyth September 2020

Introduction Update

This is a companion volume to Audrey's earlier book, 'The Wonders Of Nepal – April 1988'. In this book her journey takes place in a very different part of the world where a little known sea fronts countries of great diversity, different cultures, languages and political makeup.

Also much has changed (Note3) from 1988 when the country of Ukraine included the Crimea and it was indeed a privilege during her journey to freely visit Yalta and Sevastopol. The cruise was an ideal way to achieve this.

However, since the subsequent Crimea's annexation by Russia such opportunities are less available and Audrey's record is probably quite unique in that regard. Enjoy.

Graham Forsyth February 2021

The Black Sea- October 2008

The Black Sea is an inland sea bounded by Europe, Anatolian Turkey and the Caucasus and is ultimately connected to the Atlantic Ocean via the Mediterranean and Aegean Seas and various straits.

The Bosphorus connects it to the Sea of Marmara, and the Dardanelles connect it to the Aegean region of the Mediterranean. These waters separate Eastern Europe and western Asia and it is this melting pot of such varied cultures which make it a fascinating part of the world to explore.

The Black Sea also connects to the Sea of Azov by the Kerch Strait. This body of water is surrounded by the countries of Bulgaria, Georgia, Romania, Russia, Turkey and Ukraine all staking their claim to this vital means of transport between East and West.

It is constrained by the Pontic mountains to the South, the Caucasus to the east and features a wide shelf to the north-west – all in all, it stretches for about 1,175 km.

The Black Sea has a positive water balance i.e. there is an inflow of warm, salty seawater from the Mediterranean and an outflow of cool, freshwater from the Black Sea. This freshwater comes from the many rivers entering into the Black Sea – the main ones being the Danube, Don and Dnieper.

This makes the Sea warm and salty at the bottom and cool and fresh near the top. Strabo, the Greek geographer, reports that in antiquity, the Black Sea was just called "the Sea" and for the most part, in Greek/Roman tradition, it is referred to as the "Hospitable Sea (Euxeinos Pontos).

However, the Greek poet, Pindar states as early as the 5th century BC, that it was called the "Inhospitable Sea" before Greek colonisation as it was difficult to navigate and its shores were inhabited by savage tribes.

Another reason for the name may be an ancient assignment of colours to the cardinal directions – black referring to the north, red to the south and yellow to the east, or it could be that the Black Sea, being less salty, has a greater concentration of micro-algae causing the dark colour. Visibility in the water is approximately 5 metres compared with up to 35 metres in the Mediterranean – however the water appeared as blue as any other on a bright sunny day.

One Bulgarian theory of the name is that the sea used to be quite stormy, dating the Black Sea Deluge Theory back to Noah's Ark. The guides in each country have their own stories to tell.

The Black Sea is and has always been a busy waterway, especially in the ancient world. Marco Polo returned by this route and it is the fabled sea of the Argonauts and Colchis (now Georgia) was where Jason sought the Golden Fleece – this was the edge of the known world as far as the Greeks were concerned.

Ancient trade routes are currently being studied by scientists and archaeologists who are hoping to find prehistoric settlements along the continental shelf and perhaps ancient shipwrecks well-preserved because of the lack of oxygen in the water. Numerous ancient ports line the Black Sea's coasts, some older than the pyramids.

Thursday 2nd October 2008
Istanbul - Turkey

A quick flight from London and we were in Istanbul once more – our second time this year. We landed at a different airport though and the journey into the city was quite some distance, and on the Asian side.

Istanbul - Crossing the Bosphorus Bridge

We crossed over one of the Bosphorus Bridges and could almost see our destination for the next 10 days. We were going to join the MV Discovery on the next leg of its journey. This a medium sized ship and it's itinerary was to cruise round the coastline of the Black Sea.

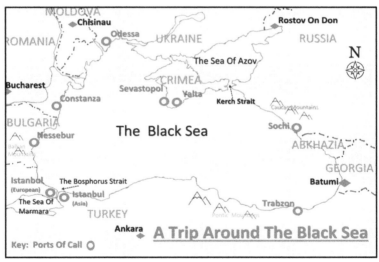

The Black Sea - Showing the ports of call

We had heard that, at this time of year, the sea could be very stormy but we were lucky and, although we had the occasional shower, the weather was exceptionally calm and sunny for this season.

We arrived at the dock just as the sun was going down, giving us a glimpse of the old city once again.

Once settled in our cabin, a very comfortable Junior suite, we set sail along the Bosphorus heading for the Black Sea. Unfortunately, the previous week Russia and Georgia had a confrontation over one of their border areas and the Russian fleet had entered a port nearby to Batumi, which was to be one of our ports of call. As we could not enter Georgia, we were to spend 2 days in Sochi, Russia instead (Note1). Our first evening was a bit of a muddle as we had requested a table for 8 and found ourselves at one for 4. However, we ended up sitting with a lovely couple from Yorkshire and after our first taste of the menu, we retired to recharge the batteries for tomorrow.

Istanbul at sunset

Friday 3rd October 2008

At Sea – Istanbul to Trabzon

Istanbul in the morning as the ship, MV Discovery,
left her mooring for the Black Sea

After breakfast on the deck outside, we were required to attend the mandatory Safety Drill, an exercise which is a requirement of law on all ships. Today was to be a day at sea and this was the time to meet the crew and our guest lecturers for the voyage. Mo Holland was the lady who was going to inform us about our ports of call and all the shore excursions. Colonel John Nowers was our military historian and, since we were to be visiting the Crimea area, he was there to give details about the Crimean War.

Finally Sir Richard Parsons, once a private secretary to Foreign Secretary George Brown and ambassador to Spain, Sweden and Hungary, who turned out to be a most amusing speaker as he gave us some political history on many of the countries as well as recounting episodes in his own ambassadorial life.

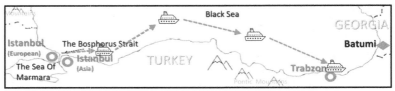

At Sea – Sailing from Istanbul to Trabzon

The 4 lectures today were about our visit to Trabzon, Turkey, our visit to Sochi, Russia, the history of the Crimean War and the political history of Turkey until Ataturk. I also managed to squeeze in a cookery demonstration by the Executive Chef Neil, an Australian, and this earned me a pen at the end of the voyage.

I have covered Turkish history on another trip and will not repeat it. Sir Richard described once again the rise of the Ottoman Empire when it was a terrifying power, to the fall when it became a joke, and how Mustafa Kemal Ataturk rose to power and united the whole of Turkey.

This was not a bloodless coup as many of the government ministers were hanged and then under the Treaty of Nozère, all Greeks were repatriated to Greece and vice versa all Turkish citizens in Greece were returned to Turkey.

This had a devastating effect on the lives of thousands of people especially those who had inter-married. Ataturk also abolished the wearing of the fez; introduced the Latin alphabet; brought back music and ballet; gave women equal rights and tried to encourage the population to become more western in dress, culture and attitude.

In 1936 there was a plot to assassinate Ataturk but the leaders were caught and hanged. Ataturk died 2 years later of cirrhosis of the liver and since then it has been a constant struggle for the government to maintain its secular ways with the rise of Islamic fundamentalism. I will discuss the other lectures when the subject arises.

After a busy day mentally and getting to know some of our fellow passengers , we attended the Captain's Welcome Reception (more champagne) and then a classical concert and off to bed to wake up at our first port early the next morning.

Saturday 4th October 2008

Trabzon – Turkey

MV Discovery docked in Trabzon

The Black Sea region of Turkey is one of the loveliest, most scenic and culturally authentic areas of the country. This is Turkey's wettest region and the climate is moist and moderate even in summer. The coastal plain rises to lush tea and hazelnut plantations, virgin forests and the Pontic Mountains, which form an almost unbroken barrier.

The local people are down to earth and industrious, especially the women. Smallholdings are common and many of the owners have retained their Caucasian traditions with Temel and Idris being popular Black Sea names, though Temel much less so.

The earliest evidence of civilisation in Trabzon dates from 7,000 BC. Located between two ravines, the elongated tableland gave the name to the city because of its shape.

Established as a Greek colony and called Trapezus, the town bene-fitted from its position on the busy trade route between the Black Sea and the Mediterranean. The first Greek explorations of the Black Sea are chronicled in the semi-legendary form as the voyages of Jason and the Argonauts, and colonisation of the south coast is attributed to the mythical Amazon female warriors.

Amazon has more recently been discovered to be an Armenian word meaning "moon women", probably referring to priestesses of a moon goddess. In 400BC the Greek Xenephon and 10,000 mercenaries fought their way out of Persia and reached Trapezus, after battling through the uncharted lands of Kurdistan and Armenia.

The city was added to the kingdom of Pontus by Mithridates IV and it became the home of the Pontic fleet. When the kingdom was annexed to the Roman Province of Galatia in 64-65BC, the fleet simply passed to the new commanders, becoming the Classis Pontica.

Trapezus gained importance under Roman rule because of a road over the Zigana Pass which led to Armenia and the Upper Euphrates valley. New roads were constructed from Persia and Mesopotamia under the rule of Vespasian and Hadrian commissioned improvements to give the city a more structured harbour.

St Andrew is said to have brought Christianity to prosperous Trabzon during his Black Sea Mission around 60AD. However, in 257AD, the town was plundered by the Goths and, although it was rebuilt, Trapezus did not recover until the trade route regained importance in the 8th -10th centuries, when it became an outpost of the Byzantine emperor.

After the crusaders sacked Constantinople (Istanbul) in 1206, the grandsons of Emperor Andronicus 1, Alexius and David Comnenus, escaped to Trebizond, as it was now called, and established a Byzantine dynasty. During the Comnene era, the city gained a reputation as a beautiful, sophisticated cultural centre. The Genoese and the Venetians came here to trade, as Trabzon was the terminus of the northern branch of the Silk route –Marco Polo returned from China by way of Trabzon.

The Comnene consolidated power through judicious foreign marriage alliances with its princesses of legendary beauty. In the medieval age of chivalry, the Comnenus princesses were of such fabled beauty that Miguel de Cervantes' hero, Don Quixote, identified the lady of his dreams as one of that exquisite elite : Dulcinea del Toboso – his Hispanified version of Trebizond.

After 250 years of exploiting these beauties as negotiating counters in their precarious diplomacy, it all came to an end when this brilliant culture and opulence ended in 1461 with Sultan Mehmet II's capture of the city, eight years after the fall of Constantinople to the Ottoman Empire.

Following this takeover, Sultan Mehmet executed all the Comnenus men but spared the ladies, keeping one of them – subsequently known as Gulbahar, "Spring rose" –for his son, the future Sultan Bayezid II. He also sent many Turkish settlers into the area, but the old ethnic Armenian, Greek and Abkhaz communities remained. During the late Ottoman period, the city had a great Christian influence in terms of culture and a wealthy merchant class, but this port became a backwater until the First World War when it was captured by forces under the command of Grand Duke Nicholas Nicolaevich the younger.

Ataturk landed near here at Samsun in 1919 to launch his War of Independence and when the Republic was formed in 1923 and the massive exchange of Greek and Turkish citizens took place – many of the wealthy merchants in Trabzon had to abandon homes and land.

During World War II, the shipping activities were limited because the Black Sea had become a battle field and as a result the most important export products, such as tobacco, hazelnuts and tea were unable to leave, so lost their value and subsequently, the living standards were affected badly.

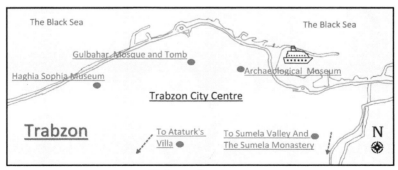

Trabzon – Location map

A new modern 4-laned highway has been built to revitalise the region and, since the fall of the Soviet Union in 1991,the frontiers of the new republics have opened up for trade – there is hardly a town in this area that does not have a Russian market filled with Russians, Tatars, Uzbeks and Kazakhs unloading their wares.

We were going on two trips here in Trabzon: the first to the Sumela Monastery and in the afternoon a visit to the old city of Trabzon itself. Our journey into the mountains was supposed to begin very early but on waking, we found the ship still not in the harbour. Apparently, the pilot had overslept and we docked later than usual.

The Sumela Monastery sits within the borders of the Altindere village of Macka district, and was built on the steep rock cliffs of Mt. Mela, precariously perched above a rockbound torrent. The monastery clings to the cliff, in this awesome location, exemplifying the classical belief that prayers said here have a shorter distance to travel to be fulfilled.

The Sumela Monastery- Initial sighting

It lies 30 miles south-east of Trabzon and our journey led us through a varied landscape of tea and tobacco plantations, fields of corn, hazelnut groves, and forests of beech, black alder, maple, oak and pines. When the road became too narrow, we had to change into a minibus to ascend 250 metres in the next 2 miles. The final part was a bracing half-hour walk over the aqueduct, which used to supply water for the monastery, and then through the forest. The climb culminated in a rock-hewn staircase leading to the main entrance with guard rooms and an interior staircase down to the main courtyard (not for the faint-hearted).

The Sumela Monastery was founded in the 4th century by two Greek monks, Barnabas and Sophronius, who were led to the site by an icon of the "Black Virgin" (Panagia Soumela) which gave rise to its present name.

Two further approaching views of the monastery

Building structure closeup

Impressive external monastery panorama view

Attributed to the Evangelist, St.Luke, the icon now rests in the museum of Athens. The monks lived in the rock cave during the time of Theodosius I and, after their death, Sumela became a place of pilgrimage, decorated with frescoes and filled with treasures including priceless manuscripts and silver plates.

On the order of Emperor Justinian, it was repaired and expanded in the 6th century by Belisarius, one of the generals of the Emperor. In the 11th century, it grew into a monastery, with 72 rooms for the guests ranged along the five-storey outside building overlooking the Altindere valley.

The external entrance staircase (down & up views)

The second staircase

During the Comnenus princedom, the monastery gained in importance and its revenues increased – one of the frescoes commemorates the coronation of Alexis II in 1340. When the Black Sea coast came under the Sovereignty of the Ottoman Sultans, the rights of Sumela were protected and given material support. A second rock-hewn staircase leads down to the main courtyard where the original cave sanctuary, several chapels, a kitchen, student rooms, guest rooms, a library and the Holy Spring are all situated.

Window view of internal quadrangle

Doorway view including doorside fresco

Internal building

Ceiling fresco

View out over the Sumela Valley

Internal fresco – Part 1

Internal fresco continuation - Part 2

During the Russian occupation and the Turkish War of Independence, the monks fled and the site suffered great damage by theft and graffiti on the frescoes. Despite the defacement by vandals ancient and modern, the frescoes surviving in the shrine still do justice to the venerable monastery. The interior and exterior walls of the cave date back to the earlier years of around the 14th Century, and are portrayals of Christ Pantocrator, the Virgin, and various Biblical stories.

Internal Buildings Constructed Inside the Front Facade

Another view of the internal buildings

External Decoration

The frescoes in the chapels date from the 18th century, however, some of them have cracked revealing older frescoes underneath which, after so many centuries, are still in magnificent condition. Close to the church is a pool (the Holy Spring) whose source is an overhanging rock. Visitors during the 19th century used to bathe in the pool whilst people today are content to drink the reputedly healing waters. (not me!).

Fresco Details

A selection of the intricate and colourful frescos

In the 19th century, apparently, Sumela had a magnificent appearance and it became the haunt for many foreign travellers, who mentioned it in their various writings. After an enjoyable visit, we made our way up and down the hazardous staircases, back through the forest and down to the coast for our lunch.

Inside one of the Sumela Monastery rooms which encloses the rock outcrop

This afternoon we were to visit some of the more important sites in Trabzon itself. Trabzon's long and eventful past was shaped by its great strategic significance to dynasties and empires throughout history. As we travelled through the city, we could see the remains of the city walls, sections of which date back to the early 5th century when Trabzon was part of the Roman Empire. Enlarged and restored during the Ottoman period, they were built as three separate sections. "Yukarihisar" – the upper fortress was the centre of the Byzantine era, "Ortahisar", the middle fortress was the centre of administration in Ottoman times and "Asagihisar", the lower fortress was the city's trade centre.

We journeyed a few kilometres outside the city centre to a district in the west to visit one of the few surviving neoclassical mansions, Kosku

Ataturkun, a dazzling white pavilion built in 1903 on a hill, overlooking the city and the Black Sea.

This house was built, in European style on three storeys, by Mr. Karaiannidis, a Greek banker. He had to leave, with all Trabzon's Greeks, during the mass Greco-Turkish exchange of Christians and Muslims, imposed by the 1923 Treaty of Lausanne.

The Ataturk White Pavilion and Gardens, Trabzon

Ataturk visited Trabzon three times in his life. On the first two visits he greatly admired the white house surrounded by the pine trees on the slopes above the city so the Trabzon municipality gave the house to Ataturk and he stayed there on his third visit in June 1937, when he wrote much of his will, the year before his death.

Today, this house is a museum to the Father of the Turkish nation and, apart from being a typical example of upper-class Crimean architecture, it houses many personal possessions and photographs from that era. Ataturk left the house to his sister Makbule Atakan at his death and although it was a family home and then a guest house, the interior has been left almost undisturbed. Outside in the driveway is a statue of Ataturk with the inscription "Hope is youth!"

The White Pavilion and nearby bust of Ataturk

Many other stately mansions, abandoned by the Greeks, can be seen in the town, and we were about to visit a second one, now the Archaeological Museum. It was built by a Greek banker, Kotsaki Teophylaktos, between 1899 and 1913 as a large family accommodation in the Baroque style.

During the Independence War, it was used as one of the headquarters and Ataturk and his family stayed there in 1924. After nationalisation, it became, in turn, the Governor's Hall, the Inspectors Headquarters and a girl's school before becoming a Museum containing displays of local archaeology and ethnography. The basement is turned into an archaeological hall with artefacts from the Bronze Age to the late Ottoman period. The first floor is given over to Islamic art, armoury, handwriting and embroideries.

Ataturk Pavilion showing balconies front and rear

Garden view from the Ataturk Pavilion front/ side balcony

Also the bedroom that was prepared for Ataturk's visit is on display, even with the original furniture. The building itself is a perfect example of Baroque and Rococo architecture at that time, with much drawing and painting on the walls and ceilings. While the outside of the building reflects Italian architecture, the woodwork inside the building signals Russian craftsmanship.

On we went next to the Gulbahar Mosque and Tomb. You may remember the name Gulbahar (Spring Rose) from the Comnenus princess captured by Sultan Mehmet for his son.

This mosque and adjacent mausoleum were built by Sultan Selim the Grim in memory of his mother, Gulbahar. This is one of the few mosques in the city that was not originally a church. It was built as part of an "imaret", an Ottoman social welfare institution consisting of a soup kitchen and hostel for students and the poor. The mosque is all that remains of the complex, with the octagonal tomb lying just to the east. Gulbahar was revered by the people of Trabzon for her pious attachment to both her Christian and adopted Muslim faith and her great charity work. Unfortunately, we could not enter this mosque as no women are allowed inside!

Up on a green slope, overlooking the sea to the west of the city centre, is the jewel of Trabzon's monuments – the 13th century Byzantine Church of Haghia Sophia. It was originally built, probably on the ruins of a Roman temple, by the Comnenus Emperor, Manuel VII Palaeologus (1238-1263).

Upper entrance stone frieze of Adam and Eve - Haghia Sophia

Miraculously surviving its metamorphoses as a mosque, ammunition dump and hospital, the church was restored in 1957 by art historians from Edinburgh University and now has the status of a museum.

Over the southern portal is a stone frieze of Adam and Eve in the Garden of Eden, carved by Black Sea artists brought in from Armenia or Georgia, with the Comnenus eagle sitting above the frieze. On the eastern side you can see figures of mythological characters such as centaurs, griffons and pigeon motifs.

Arch Design

Coloured Decoration

Column Example

Horse Head Design

Of superior workmanship, the stone reliefs reflect not only the influence of Christian art, but also that of Islamic art. Medallions decorated with interlocking geometric designs bear the characteristics of carvings of the Seljuk period. The interior walls are adorned with splendid frescoes of biblical scenes and are among the finest examples of Byzantine painting.

The Comnenus Eagle - Sculpture Detail

Column Heading Decoration

The frescoes in the narthex (entrance hall) depict scenes from the life of Jesus, while those in the north porch are devoted to the Old Testament stories, notably the tribulations of Job. In the dome, the usual Christ Pantocrator has been obliterated but his surrounding angels and apostles are still vividly present. In the apse, frescoes portray the Ascension above the Virgin Enthroned, flanked by archangels. The patterned mosaics date from Byzantine times, and you can still see the original coloured marble covering of the floor. Outside the church is an Italian style campanile which was added in 1427 and was regularly used as a lighthouse. At the western door are many carved animal statues dating from a much earlier period and, strangely, an old cannon left behind by the Russians when it was an arsenal.

Venetian Graffiti

41

Sunk into the grassy slope towards the sea are the stone remains of a baptismal font and, as we walked round the building, we were amazed to see some medieval graffiti on the external walls. The outlines of boats and dates have been scratched into the stonework probably by the Venetians, the historians believe.

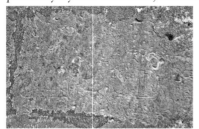

Additional Venetian Graffiti

At the end of our first sight-seeing day we returned to the ship to be welcomed in our room with a selection of canapés and champagne – this was to be a daily decadence, I'm afraid. Our meal this evening was to be dishes from around the world as was the show later on.

Overnight Sailing – Trabzon to Sochi

Sunday 5th October 2008

Sochi – Russia

Sochi is situated on Russia's southern Black Sea coastline in the western foothills of the Caucasus Mountain Range close to the border. The close proximity of the big Caucasian Ridge and warm Black Sea produces a subtropical climate making Sochi the most northern subtropics in the world. It extends in ribbon development for 90 miles along the coast and is claimed to be the longest city in Europe.

The city has been selected to be the host to the 22nd Winter Olympic Games in 2014.

Sochi Harbour Panorama

In 800 BC the Scythians from central Asia drove the Cimmerians (probably Iranians) out of the Black Sea region and along with Greek merchants set up trading posts.

The brief Roman presence from the 1st century was succeeded by waves of nomadic warriors – Huns, Khazars and Arabs. Christianity spread from Constantinople in the 10th century but then, there was the Mongol invasion of Genghis Khan (1223,) and this was extended to the Black Sea by his grandson, Batu.

Many Tatars settled here and converted to Islam in the 14th century, and when there was fear of a new Russian threat from Ivan the Terrible, the region was annexed and came under the sovereignty of the Ottoman Empire. Led by Catherine the Great and her successors in the Russo-Turkish Wars, the Black Sea coastline was eventually ceded to Russia in 1829 but the Russians had no detailed knowledge of the area until Baron Fyodor Tornau secretly investigated the coastal route in the 1830's.

In 1838, the fort of Alexandria, renamed Navaginsky, was founded at the mouth of the Sochi River and a chain of fortifications was set up to protect the area. At the outbreak of the Crimean War, the fort was evacuated in order to prevent capture by the Turks who landed on Cape Adler nearby.

After the war, most of the Circassians were forced to relocate to Turkey, leaving the area largely depopulated but the coast was soon resettled by Russians, Armenians and Greeks, and the burgeoning settlement was renamed Sochi after the local river.

In the last Tsarist years, the first construction of hotels, mansions and sanatoria appeared, turning Sochi into a seaside health resort. During the Russian Revolution, the coastline saw sporadic clashes involving the Red Army, the White Movement forces and the Democratic Republic of Georgia. In 1923, Sochi acquired one of its most distinctive features – a railway running along the coast to Abkhazia.

Although this branch of the North Caucasus Railway may appear incongruous, in the setting of beaches and sanatoriums, it is still operational and vital to the region's transportation infrastructure. Sochi was established as a fashionable resort under Joseph Stalin, who had his favourite dacha (country cottage) in the city. At that time the coast became dotted with Neo-classical edifices and clinics catering in most to the Party Apparatchiks but there were also workers' sanitoria for the most deserving. More recently this was a favourite place of Boris Yeltsin and Vladimir Putin has just built a new dacha here.

We were told on arrival that the passport control would be difficult and serious but I passed through this system 6 times and it was quick and efficient, and by the end, I managed to make the girl smile with my halting Russian. We did not require a personal visa for this short trip which made things easier.

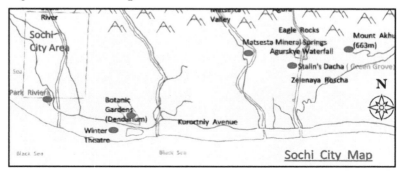

We met our guide, Marianna, who took us for a walk along the "Park Riviera", which is a long pedestrian esplanade running parallel to the sea. We could see many fine buildings from the beginning of the 20th century, and much new building construction. In recent years, a large amount of money has been allocated to Sochi, probably because of the forthcoming Winter Olympics.

The Sochi Park Riviera

This must be a very busy place in the summer months with the open-air theatres and all the cafes. In town, is a profusion of exotic trees, shrubs and tropical plants, flourishing in public parks and private gardens.

Sochi - Waterfront

The town boasts a Botanical Garden, called the Dendarium, which was laid out at the end of the 19th century and displays over 1,500 trees and shrubs from all over the world.

There is also an Arboretum, where the major attraction is "The Tree of Friendship", planted in 1934, amidst citrus trees on which grafts of over 140 different species have sprouted, including a Japanese mandarin, an American orange, an Italian lemon and Indian grapefruit.

The impressive Winter Theatre

The Sochi Waterfront - Promenade

At the end of the esplanade stands the Winter Theatre, seating 400 people, a neoclassical building, having 88 perimeter Greek Corinthian columns, with a pediment bearing the statues of Terpsichore, Melpomene and Thalia, three of the Muses, of dance, tragedy and comedy.

We also saw an old cannon dredged up from the sea, probably a relic of Russia's 19th century battles with the Ottoman navy. Our final building was the oldest building in Sochi –the Alexander Pushkin Library, which was small but very attractive and closed!

Sochi Lenin statue Surrounded by Sub-Tropical foliage

On to the coach now and along past Lenin's significant statue, we were heading to the outskirts to visit Stalin's dacha. The journey was short but on our way we could see the disparity in housing –some were beautiful stone built mansions, but many were large bleak Stalinist housing blocks and there were also wooden shacks roofed with corrugated iron and in a very poor condition.

On top of the mountain range between the Matsestinskaya Valley and the Agura Canyon there is a mysterious green castle. It is the former dacha of Joseph Stalin in Sochi, "Zelenaya Roscha" (The Green Grove).

Built in the 1930's, it is situated within an old forest park, which, before the revolution, was the "Mikhailovskoe Estate", belonging to the famous Russian manufacturer and tea-trader, Mikhail Zenzinov.

Stalin's Dacha – Zelenaya Roscha - The Green Grove

Other External Views of the Dacha

It was nationalised in 1918 and some cottages on the estate were put into order for the leaders of the newly founded Soviet Union to come there on holiday.

In January 1924, ten days after the death of Vladimir Lenin, a secret meeting of the Central Committee of the Communist Party of the Soviet Union (Bolsheviks) was held in Moscow.

A question about "Health protection of the party leaders" was under consideration. As a result, a special medical department was founded developing "Kremlin hospitals", polyclinics and pharmacies and, at the same time, a department of health resorts was set up.

When Stalin became the General Secretary of the Central Committee, his powers grew and he became a man not to be contradicted. The city of Sochi was declared to be one of the main objects of the first five-year plan.

Sanatorium buildings were constructed, a beautiful Winter Theatre and a magnificent house for the Commissioner (now the Art Museum) appeared. At the same time, Stalin had four holiday dachas built, his favourite being at Zelenaya Roscha.

External Façade - Zelenaya Roscha - The Green Grove

In 1932, a young architect Miron Merzhanov was chosen to build the dacha and this resulted in many other commissions such as his other dachas, the Greater Kremlin Palace and a famous Congress Hall. At that time, he could consider himself the best architect in the country but as all Soviet people found out, including Stalin's best friends, he could suddenly decide that he no longer needed their services and poor Merzhanov was eventually slandered, convicted and spent 12 years in prison – he was one of the lucky ones. To decorate the dacha walls and ceilings, in the rooms precious species of wood were used and which are still in perfect order.

Stalin's Bed

Stalin's Cinema Room

The main building contained Stalin's study, his bedroom, rooms for his assistants and for his son and daughter.

On the second floor there is a very beautiful hall with a fireplace where dinners were held and in the adjoining building was his billiard room and a cinema hall - as Stalin was known to watch every film that was issued in order to decide if it was suitable for his people.

There was a pool in the basement, but this was never used as Stalin had a dreadful phobia about drowning in water. A story to illustrate this is: just before he was due to visit the first time, the architect had a small patio with an elegant fountain constructed in front of the house.

When the head of the guard came to make a preliminary inspection, he stamped his feet shouting: "Take it away immediately! The master can't bear fountains!" In one night, the fountain disappeared, and a smart flower bed took its place by the morning.

Stalin became a leader whose every whim was fulfilled with just the wave of his hand because everyone was so afraid of his power.

Once, when the governmental motorcade was rushing along, he did not like that the guard along the road included militia sergeants. "Make them all Lieutenants," he ordered.

And everybody, even the most semi-literate guards were given officers' salaries, rations and privileges. On another occasion Stalin pulled a face when he had glanced at the new building of the Red Army sanatorium built in constructivist style.

"Build two palaces to the left and right" he instructed and made them a present to the working class. And it was done – the Ordzhonikidze sanatorium in classical style with porticoes and columns was given for the Miners and Metallurgists rest.

Stalin was also paranoid about safety for himself. The dacha was painted green to blend in with the forest, in order to hide it from air attack; he had guards standing every 15 metres round the perimeter fence and escape tunnels were located under the building.

This place had an odd feeling because of the circumstances that had occurred there. It was from here that he made some dreadful decisions; he sent ciphered telegrams to Moscow sending thousands to their death or exile, and he plotted with friends who would also receive the same fate. In the years of perestroika, in the Sochi Art Museum, there was an exhibition devoted to Stalin's prisons.

The pictures on display were mediocre but there was no one emotionally indifferent in the hall to them. In the comments book of wishes and references side by side were written diametrically opposed opinions of Joseph Stalin.

Many wrote about their hatred of the dictator, because they had lost relatives in the purges or because of the thousands who died of starvation. Others were indignant about the slanders made against the leader who saved them from fascism.

One veteran just wrote two numbers of five figures – the first was his personal number in Buchenwald, the second –in Russian prison, in Kolima but , on the same page, in red ink, was written the famous quotation of Winston Churchill; "Stalin took Russia with the plough, but left it with the atomic weapon".

Our guide taking us around the dacha was Anna, who only spoke Russian, so there was a lot of translation necessary although I understood a remarkable amount. She told us most of the above information, and that Russian people came here for two reasons; one was to spit on the ground because of their hatred or else to venerate a man they considered a great leader – Russia is still divided on this point.

Stalin's desk in the study

Stalin's Sideboard

The billiard room in the dacha

Balcony adjoining the dictator's accommodation

View through one of the dacha windows

The main part of the dacha is now an exclusive hotel and spa but the smaller building has been turned into a small museum. After thirty years of oblivion, after Stalin's death, very little was found – a leather divan, where Stalin would sit and talk with his guests, the billiard table still with the burns left by his cigars and a silver inkwell, given as a present from Mao Tse Tung on his 70th birthday.

A bed, a desk, some chairs and some family photographs are all that remain here. In the film room his desk, bed and divan are set up with a wax model of "the people's leader" sitting at the desk.

Painting of Stalin   *Yalta Conference photo (centre)*

Official painting of Stalin above a fireplace

Stalin was a very small man and he had his furniture made in such a way that it made him appear taller. There were photographs of his first wife, Ekaterina Svanidze, and his second wife, Nadezhda Alliluyeva, and also his son Vasily and daughter Svetlana.

There is no picture of his first son, Jakov, whom he did not even see for the first 15 years of his life and who later died in a German prisoner-of-war camp.

His son, Vasily, was an idle drunkard, who passed no exams but still became a colonel in the army. His much-loved daughter, Svetlana, wrote a book "Twelve Letters to a Friend "about their time in Sochi.

However, the relationship between Stalin and his daughter became strained as she grew up and she realised what was happening. In a second room was the billiard table and a large chess set, two games Stalin enjoyed, as long as he won.

After our talk here, we were taken round the main building and eventually to the large dining room with its vaulted ceiling which was just as it had always been.

Vaulted ceiling room that served as
Stalin's main meeting room / formal reception room / dining room

There I stood with a glass of champagne, eating blinis with smoked salmon and caviar, while the large portrait of Stalin glowered down over the proceedings.

As I looked out of the window to the sun shining in the lovely garden and nearby forest, I could not stop thinking of the other people who had stood here before me.

Names such as Molotov, Voroshilov, Yagoda and Lavrentiy Beriya conjured up pictures which sent shivers up my spine as I recalled the terror these men had a hand in creating and by which many had perished themselves. It was a lovely sunny morning but we left this visit with many questions and mixed feelings.

Our next stop was the Matsesta Valley mineral springs. Roman colonists who lived in Dioscuria, the city which stood on the shores of Sukhumi bay, called the path to Matsesta – "the path of the lucky springs" and many Greek, Roman and Ottoman dignitaries came here to try the waters.

The valley's name means "fiery water" because the skin is reddened by the sulphurous springs, rich in sodium chloride and 26 other minerals –good for rheumatism, skin ailments and gynaecological problems.

Matsesta Entrance Sign

People have long known of the mineral waters' curative properties and used to treat themselves. Initially, they simply dug holes near the spring, poured the water inside and had baths.

Matsesta Sanitorium Entrance

Matsesta Sanitorium Building

In 1902, Dr. Podgurskiy started a development of the spa facilities at the Matsesta sulphur springs which gained in popularity because of the successful treatments.

We looked at the huge classical building which is now the Sanatorium and then walked round to the rock caves where the actual spring forces its way through the rocks.

Cave Entrance

Sulphur Pools

We were told of the legend of the girl looking for water for her parents and being captured by an evil spirit whom she had to marry but later killing him and setting the water free for all.

Every ancient site has its legends but there is always a grain of truth if you look hard enough. After a very full morning, we returned to the ship for lunch.

This afternoon we were to visit one of the most beautiful parts of Sochi, namely Dagomys, Russia's Tea Capital and also a favourite place of Vladimir Putin to entertain guests.

Russian Samovar

In 1896, a delegation of Russians returned from a distant voyage to China bringing with them the seeds of exquisite Chinese tea. These were planted in a Georgian settlement near Batumi where only 5% of the seeds proved to have a germinating capacity – the wily Chinese had scalded the tea. Five years later, however, the first Russian plantation appeared in Sochi and today, the only area of tea farms in Russia, is the northernmost commercial tea producer in the world. We travelled along the Black Sea coastline and then up into the hills where we had stunning views of the sea, the town of Sochi and the snow-capped Caucasus Mountains from the slopes of Mount Armyanka.

Russian Tea Plants

Tea Plantations on the Caucasus

A guide explained about the plantations, the type of tea and the use of the samovar, while we sat in the sunshine overlooking the fields and mountains.

Tea pantation management explained

Dagomy's Tea Chalet

Tea plantations here produce what's considered to be Russia's best brew, Krasnoda, which we were about to taste from the samovar in a traditional ornate glass.

We walked up to the tea chalet, an amazing building in itself, and were greeted by ladies in traditional costume who seated us at the wooden tables inside. Preparing Russian tea is a special ceremony.

Individual tea room   *Singers in Russian dress*

Ethnic folk art tea room

Tea Chalet Ground Floor Interior

Musical Accompaniment to the Tea Drinking

Tea Drinking – Russian Style

First, boiling water from the samovar is used to brew a very strong concentrated tea in a special small porcelain tea pot. The tea is then prepared by filling your cup from the samovar and then adding the brewed concentrate to taste – no milk is added.

Then you are ready to drink and toast: "Pej na Zdrovije!" (Drink for your health!) The tea was very good and our table was laden with hazelnuts, plum and fig jam, honey and home-made breads - absolutely delicious.

While we enjoyed our afternoon tea, we were entertained by a singing, dancing family folk group. The star turn was the father who played a range of balalaikas and accordions down to the tiniest little thing from which he still managed to produce a melodic sound.

Ethnic Folk Art on Display

The chalet was entirely made of wood with lots of little rooms set for smaller tea parties and the walls were covered with paintings of very colourful ethnic folk art. This had been a very enjoyable way to spend the afternoon and I still can't believe I was standing looking at the Caucasus.

One of the Smaller Tea Rooms

This evening on board was to be a Russian dinner. Russian cuisine derives its rich and varied character from the vast and multicultural expanse of nations. Its foundations were laid by the peasant food of the rural population with a combination of plentiful fish, poultry, game, mushrooms, berries and honey.

Crops of rye, wheat, barley and millet provided ingredients for a plethora of breads, pancakes, cereals, Kvass, beer and vodka.

From the time of Catherine the Great, however, every family of note imported products and chefs from mainly Germany, Austria and France which makes many dishes we consider to be Russian, actually Franco-Russian from the 18th and 19th centuries – such as Beef Stroganoff, Chicken Kiev and Sharlotka (Charlotte Russe).

Shchi (cabbage soup) had been the main first course in Russian cuisine for over a thousand years. Although tastes have changed, it steadily made its way through several epochs. Shchi knew no social class boundaries, and even if the rich had richer ingredients and the poor made it solely of cabbage and onions, all these "poor" and "rich" variations were cooked in the same tradition.

The unique taste of this cabbage soup was from the fact that after cooking it was left to stew in a Russian stove.

Borshcht is another famous Russian soup, made with beetroot, and we enjoyed a plate of that at the meal.

After dinner, because we were staying for another day, a local group of singers and dancers came on board to give a show and we were able to watch it on deck because it was such a lovely evening.

Monday 6th October 2008

Sochi – Russia

Russian Beer Advertisement passed enroute to Mount Akhun

We were blessed with such beautiful weather yesterday but today we woke up to thick fog and heavy drizzle. Unfortunately today our visit was to a famed viewpoint – Mount Akhun. 663 metres above sea level, the tower of Mount Akhun gives unparalleled views over the National Park, the Greater Caucasian range, the resort of Sochi and the Black Sea. We saw absolutely nothing!

The mountain is easily recognised because it is the highest in this area and it has a cone shape typical of volcanoes although this mountain has no history of volcanic action.

Mount Akhun Observation Tower

The observation tower on top of the mountain was built in 1936 (architect Sergei Vorobyov).

The Foggy View of the Caucasus from the Tower

The Mount Akhun Coffee Shop

The Tower's austere lines resemble early medieval Roman structures and the five-floored tower is made of limestone and marl quarried from the mountain itself. A narrow observation platform can be reached by an external staircase and we climbed to the very top but still saw nothing.

We had to use our imagination and fortunately we had seen the vast expanse of the Caucasus mountains, gorges and waterfalls the previous day.

*Mount Akhun Tower - Coffee Shop , Colourful Animal Carvings Display
and Local Merchandise Shop*

A part of this landscape are the Eagle Rocks, white with limestone, they lie along the right bank of the Agura river, close to the Agura waterfalls. Here, there are huge stone cliffs made of grey limestone and yellow sandstone, hanging right over the precipice and surprisingly, in some places, pines, oaks and hornbeams cling to the tiny ledges.

Several caves are located near Eagle rocks and the largest one has a depth of 15 metres. This area is full of myth and legend, being one of the first places the Greeks reached in their early travels. Here Jason searched for the Golden Fleece meeting Cyclops, the one-eyed giant in one of the caves.

The story of Prometheus originates here also. He is the man who stole fire from the Gods to give to the people, but, after such an offence, Zeus sent an order for him to be chained to one of the Caucasian peaks. Every day a huge eagle flew up here to peck at the liver of the unfortunate prisoner.

A second local story is about a beautiful girl Agura, who brought water to her lover chained to the rocks without her father's knowledge. When the girl's secret was discovered, she was thrown into the precipice, and striking against the stones, she turned into a mountain river running at the feet of her beloved.

Another tale tells of the girl Agura, a sister, whose brothers go off to war and are killed. She cries so much that the river Agura appears and the mountains on either side are her brothers returned to protect her.

Following the course of the river Khosta to where the valley widens, we then entered a park in which lies a primeval forest.

Box Tree Foliage   *Agura River Valley*

The Yew and Box Tree Grove is part of the Caucasian National Reserve. The ancient beauty of the place is truly enchanting with the crowns of the trees obstructing the sunshine (not today) and light green tufts of moss hanging down from gnarled branches.

I have to correct myself, as the sun began to creep gradually from behind the clouds and the warmth created a misty atmosphere and enhanced the strong smell of fallen leaves.

The Box Tree (Buxus sempervirens) is an evergreen tree with small leaves which we usually see in the form of miniature clipped hedges. The Yew Tree usually lives 500-600 years, but at 30 metres high and 2,000 years old, there is a magnificent yew tree here and also a 400 year old giant beech to impress us.

The area used to be the private hunting ground of princes as it is rich in wild life, especially wild boars, but it was subsequently declared a Reserve in the 1930's. In the heart of the grove, there are ruins of an ancient fortress from the 11th or 12th century but the history of this is, as yet, unknown.

Walking through the The Yew and Box Tree Grove within the Caucasian National Reserve

This was a very pleasant, calm way to spend the morning and the weather was improving.

As we returned to Sochi, we were assailed with tales of the original local people, the Adygian tribe, who have passed down language and customs, which still exist today.

I will recount a few of these : if someone was struck by lightning then the whole family was considered sacred: if you praised some possession of family then you were presented with the article as a gift therefore it was unwise and discourteous to praise a weapon or a horse as these were too important for survival; it was also unwise to ask after the health of a wife and they thought it honourable to sell their daughters to the Turkish harem.

Many of the population were cattle breeders, beekeepers and pirates, the two former occupations still being prevalent to this day.

St Michaels Orthodox Church

Returning to the town of Sochi, we took our last look at the Arboretum, the Dendarium , the gold, yellow, white and blue of the Winter Theatre, the Summer Theatre, and we saw the First Orthodox Church, St. Michaels, which we had missed the day before.

It was constructed between 1874 and 1891 and, as we sailed off after lunchtime, we passed the Sochi lighthouse which was built about the same time in 1890.

In the afternoon we had 2 more lectures on ports of call, Sevastopol and Odessa. These were very informative and helped in our decision surrounding what to visit when we arrived in a new port.

Sir Richard Parsons gave a humorous talk about Ukraine –the Borderland and told us stories of some of his own personal dealings with the Russians. Tonight was an American themed meal and a Wild West show to follow.

Did you Know?

- Women of the 17th Century Tsarist court were not allowed to see strangers and were secluded in the Terem, a palace for noblewomen within the Kremlin.
- There they attended religious services, embroidered and ate. The full, rounded figure was much admired.

- Royal children learned from "fun" books, colourful encyclopaedias illustrated by the most talented Kremlin artists.

- Under Alexei Mikhailovich, the second Romanov Tsar, the accidental omission of even a single word of the Tsar's lengthy titles could reap severe punishment.

- Peter the Great was 6ft 8in feet tall at a time when most people were considerably shorter than they are today.

- Piotr Alexeivich (Peter the Great) not only visited the West, he worked in it. Travelling incognito, he spent several months labouring in Dutch and English dockyards.

- The Russian Orthodox Church is over 1,000 years old. The Russian word for peasant, "krestyanin", means "a Christian".

- The word "icon" comes from the Greek "eikon", meaning "an image." Orthodox icons were created for prayer and the artist was expected to be a Christian of high moral principle who prepared for his work by fasting and praying.

- Salt was rare in ancient times and its importance was reflected in the bread and salt ceremony when visiting emperors were presented with a loaf of bread and a container of salt. The folk custom is still practiced today.

- After he peacefully freed 20-million serfs in 1861, Alexander II became known as the "Tsar Emancipator."

- On Jan. 1, 1863, Abraham Lincoln freed 200,000 slaves with his signing of the Emancipation Proclamation.

- The longest railway in the world is the Trans-Siberian Railway or Trans-Siberian Railroad, built 1891-1916, a network of railways connecting European Russia with Russian Far East provinces. It is 9,288.2 kilometres (5,787 miles) long and spans 8 time zones.

- During the time of Peter the Great, any Russian man who had a beard was required to pay a special tax.

- Russian interest in the Black Sea extends over more than two centuries. Catherine the Great annexed the Crimea in 1783 and subsequently established a Russian naval base and Black Sea Fleet at Sevastopol.

- Ukraine and Russia recently signed an agreement allowing the Russians to continue to use the base.
- Among Russia's many contributions to science and technology are Mendeleyev's Periodic Table of the Elements and the "Sputnik" space flights.
- "No dinner without bread," goes the Russian saying. Russians eat more rye bread than any nation in the world.
- Their cuisine is famous for exotic soups, cabbage schi and solyanka, which is made of assorted meats.

Tuesday 7ᵗʰ October 2008
Yalta Ukraine (Note3)

The Crimean Peninsula between the Black Sea and the Sea of Azov is often compared to the French Riviera. Sheltered from the cold north winds by the Crimean mountains, Yalta has a mild climate and spectacular scenery.

The peninsula was settled in the Stone Age and over the centuries, many different peoples have arrived. The most obvious were the Taurians, a belligerent tribe, the Scythians, who lived in the Crimea for around 700 years, and the Greeks who built several cities, among them Kalamata (Sebastopol) and Chersonesos, where trade and culture flourished. Waves of conquerors attacked the area over the centuries, including the Romans Goths, Byzantines and Slavs.

In 988, Grand Duke Vladimir of Kiev took possession of Chersonesos and was baptised there, laying the foundations for the Russian Orthodox Church. The Genoese settled along the coast after the Byzantines and then, the bloody campaigns of the Mongol Tatars destroyed their prosperity.

Chersonesos withstood foreign invasion until 1399 when it was devastated by the Golden Horde, part of the Mongol Empire, and never rebuilt. The Crimean Khanate was established in the mid-15ᵗʰ Century, with Bakhchisaray as its capital, and was maintained as a protectorate of the Ottoman Sultan for 300 years.

One of Russia's greatest aims was to gain access to the Black Sea, and this led to several Russo -Turkish wars. Catherine the Great cracked down on the Ukrainian autonomy, deposed the Khan and annexed the Crimea to the Tsardom in 1783.

In 1784 Prince Potemkin built and fortified Sebastopol as a naval port and, still today, this is where the Russian naval fleet is stationed and remains of great importance to Russia. During the Crimean War (1853- 56), the Russians fought against the British, French and Ottoman Turks and Sevastopol was besieged for 349 days and then completely destroyed after only 70 years of existence.

The Russian novelist, Leo Tolstoy joined the fighting during this dreadful war and wrote eye-witness accounts in three stories. At the time of the Bolshevik Revolution, Yalta became part of the Crimean Soviet Socialist Republic but during World War II, the peninsula was occupied by German armed forces from July 1942 to May 1944, when it was recaptured by the Red Army, entailing great losses.

Several hundred thousand Crimean Tatars and Crimean Germans, in fact all residents of the Crimea, were accused of being German collaborators and subsequently deported by Stalin to Siberia, in appalling conditions. Russians, Ukrainians, White Russians and others settled in the peninsula and in 1954, Nikita Khrushchev handed it to the Soviet Republic of Ukraine.

After the collapse of the Soviet Union in 1991, Ukraine and also incorporating the Crimean Peninsula became independent. A struggle, however, broke out between Ukraine and the Russian Federation for the ownership of the Black Sea Fleet and finally it was divided up between them.

The contract of 1997 allows the Russian Navy to remain in the port of Sevastopol until 2017, in exchange for a substantial annual sum; Russia also obtains the right to station aeroplanes, tanks and troops on Ukrainian soil. This is still a bone of contention to this very day and with their new President, there will probably be a new agreement reached before time runs out. (See Note3).

Yalta exhales a distinct air of past grandeur in the elegant colonnaded white mansions where the 19th century Russian aristocrats had their seaside houses.

At the turn of the 19th century, Yalta was still quite a small village only reachable by ship but when it became linked by road to the metropolis of Sevastopol and when the Tsar built his imperial palace at Livadia, its popularity soared, especially in September, ie the "velvet season", named so because the aristocracy all wore velvet at this time.

Many celebrated artists, musicians, writers and personalities stayed here, including Tolstoy, Chekhov, Gorky and Tchaikovsky. Virtuosos like Chaliapin and Rachmaninoff gave recitals in Yalta and in 1867 the globe-trotting Mark Twain visited.

Overnight Sailing – From Sochi to Yalta

Yalta Berth - Musical Welcome

75

In communist times, the Kremlin leaders built themselves dachas in the hills, where they went for relief from the political pressures in Moscow and the mansions were expropriated and turned into hotels and sanatoria for TB to accommodate the patients and workers sent here to recover from less favoured climates. With the collapse of the Soviet Union, however, Yalta turned again to its Ukrainian roots. We began our visit by stopping at Alexander Nevsky Cathedral built in 1902 to the design of A.Krasnov, a local architect. This is a soaring Russian Orthodox Cathedral with the most beautiful onion domes whilst its facade displays a mosaic of the ancient Prince Alexander Nevsky, who was once the supreme ruler of Russia.

Prince Alexander Nevsky Mosaic

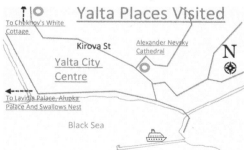

Yalta - Location Map – Places visited

The cathedral was built with money collected by the local people over a 10 year period to commemorate the death of Tsar Alexander II who was killed by a terrorist bomb in 1881. The Tsar had bought land and built the Livadia Palace nearby and was well known in the area. In 1891 the first block of the cathedral was laid by his widow, Empress Maria Fedorovna, with Alexander III in attendance.

Prince Alexander Nevsky Cathedral

We drove along the coast to the extraordinary Palace at Alupka, an outstanding monument of history and architecture. This palace was built for Count Mikhail Vorontsov, as a country residence when he was Governor- General in Odessa. After a long and distinguished military career, fighting in the Caucasus and then against Napoleon, Vorontsov, by then a Lieutenant- General in the Russian army, became Governor- General of Novo-Russia, which included the Crimea.

The Alupka (Vorontsov)

Vorontsov Coat Of Arms
Palace Entrance Archway

He followed the example of the Duc de Richilieu, Odessa's first administrator, making Odessa his working base, but establishing a private villa on the Black Sea coast at Alupka.

This Russian Count commissioned an English architect to design a palace that combined Scottish and English Gothic along with Moorish architecture – it's hard to think of a more unlikely combination for a successful building but it did succeed with remarkable elegance.

The Alupka Palace Northern Façade - Front Courtyard and Alupka Entrance Door

Room furniture

The Blue Drawing Room Piano

Exquisite Wood and Metalwork

Count Mikhail Vorontsov

Vorontsov Family Crest

Persian Room Carpet   *Dining Room Table*

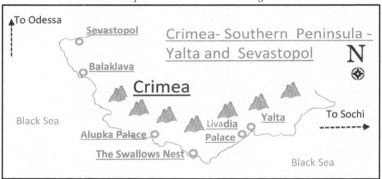

Location Map – Alupka Palace, Livadia Palace, and the Swallows Nest

Chintz Room Moorish Chandelier   *Dining Room Window Aspect*

The Winter Garden With French Windows Opening on to the Summer Garden

The architect was Edward Blore, one of the most well-known British architects of the 19th century – responsible for parts of Buckingham and St. James' Palaces in London, and for a number of other buildings in both England and Scotland.

He was a personal friend of Sir Walter Scott and had a keen interest in the architecture of Scottish castles. Count Vorontsov's father had been the Russian Ambassador in London for over 20 years and so the young Vorontsov had been raised and educated in England and was familiar with British architectural styles. His sister was also married to Lord Pembroke. The plot of land was bought in 1820 and work began in 1828 and lasted through to 1846.

The poet, Pushkin, once called Vorontsov boring and pedestrian and, as if to prove him wrong, the palace was built in a triumph of imagination. Vorontsov was, typically, fully involved in the project at every stage, and carefully discussed the details of the planned design with Edward Blore's site architect, William Hunt. The south face of the palace looks out across the Black Sea towards Turkey, and combines Russian and Moorish elements into a uniquely elegant building standing out against the Ai-Petri Mountain. The north side, on the other hand, could easily be mistaken for a Scottish castle in the Gothic tradition.

South Façade Vestibule

One thousand serfs, belonging to Vorontsov, came to work on the construction and all of those who took part were liberated when it was complete. The price for the house was 9 million silver roubles and 8 million silver roubles for the parkland.

Winter Garden Southern Façade ie Facing the Black Sea

*The Southern Façade (Cont'd) with its Oriental Appearance
and Mosque-like Vestibule and Lion Terrace*

The Palace's interior can rival the exterior in splendour of decor and this includes the Tudor-style Dining Hall complete with Minstrel's Gallery, the Blue Drawing Room with its white grand piano, the Main Study and the Winter Garden Conservatory with rare plants and statues. Many concerts were held here and once when Feodor Chaliapin, the great opera star, came with Rachmaninov accompanying him on the piano, his voice was so strong and the room was so crowded that he had to stand outside on the Terrace to perform.

Roof Top Elevation   *Medici Lions line the Stone Stair*

Palace End Façade

In the corner of the Main Study stood a cabinet, one of the many original pieces of furniture left.

In this cabinet, it was purported that the Countess Vorontsova, who was a god-daughter of Catherine the Great, kept a casket containing the secret marriage certificate of Catherine the Great and Prince Potemkin, her lover.

Southern Façade Facing Tiered Garden

Southern Façade Facing Tiered Garden Sea View

Whether this is true or not, we will never know as the revolutionaries threw all papers and documents into the sea.

The palace stands in a huge old park, with fine views of the mountains and the sea and contains fountains, ponds, cascades, terraces, staircases and many sculptures.

From the south portico, a grand staircase, called the "Terrace of Lions", with leonine statuary carved from Carrara marble – copies of the lions on Pope Clement XII's tomb in Rome – leads down to the sea.

An Onion Domed Church Viewed from the Garden and Half Hidden in The Parkland

One of the Bonani Lions

The Terrace leading to the Steps

The six famous white lions were by the Italian sculptor Bonani, who also contributed marble sculptures to the Capitol building in Washington, USA.

One of these lions is named the "Churchill Lion", as Winston Churchill was reputed to have said that that particular lion resembled him.

This was at the time when Churchill and the British delegation stayed here at the Alupka Palace during the Yalta Conference in 1945.

Two of the six Lions - One ever watchful   *and the other clearly not*

The Little Dacha in Winter Oil Painting

Walking down the hill from this lovely palace, we met a lady from Moscow, obviously fallen on hard times, who was selling her own small oil paintings. We admired one in particular of her little dacha in winter and painted on the only medium she had − a piece of plywood. She had painted it beautifully and we were very pleased with our purchase −it hangs in the lounge now.

Although it was only 10:30 in the morning, our next visit was to taste wines at the famous Massandra winery. Over the course of the last century, this vineyard has produced some of the finest wines to have emerged and survived some of the most turbulent events in history.

Winery Entrance Sign   *A purchase made – Massandra Port Wine*

The Massandra Winery was built between 1894 and 1897, primarily to cater for Tsar Nicholas II and his court. The Romanovs came every year to their Summer palace at Livadia, near Yalta and they demanded the highest quality wines. Prince Lev Golitzyn, an immensely gifted winemaker, was appointed to oversee the production at the winery.

He planted vines that suited the climate and he was an excellent blender, resulting in an unparalleled collection of sweet wines, including Muscat and Tokay and the Tsar's favourite tipple, the Livadia Red Port, that he used to decant into a small hip-flask and keep hidden in the top of his boot.

The Massandra Collection, which included hundreds of thousands of bottles of wine from all over Europe, as well as the local products, could easily have been destroyed in the bloodshed and brutality of the years following the Russian Revolution.

The Crimea was a stronghold of the anti-Bolshevik White Army and they decided to make their last stand here in 1920. In a desperate bid to protect the wine collection, the tunnels to Massandra's cellars were bricked up. It had taken 3 years to create seven tunnels up to 50 metres below ground level with miners digging 150 metres back into the hillside. The wine remained undiscovered until the Red Army finally took control of the area.

Stalin was so impressed by the wine when he tried it that he ordered it to be preserved and production at the winery resumed. He also ensured that the wine at the Tsar's other palaces, in Moscow and St. Petersburg, be moved to Massandra.

Twenty years later, the collection was once again jeopardised by the Nazi invasion of the Soviet Union. Everything had to be packed up and taken to three separate secret locations. The directors of the winery were so determined that the Nazis should not get their hands on so much as a drop of the wine that the entire 1941 vintage – which still sat in vats – was poured into the Black Sea. The wine remained secreted away until 1944, when it was reunited with the winery just in time to witness the Yalta Conference between the Allied Forces.

Despite enjoying a more harmonious existence since, life at Massandra was threatened again in 1986 when President Gorbachev imposed a wide-ranging anti-alcohol campaign. Alcohol has always been an integral part of Russian life, but the social cost of heavy drinking had become increasingly apparent. Such was the strength of feeling that a large number of vines at Massandra were torn up and production was, once again, stemmed for a time. A tale of endurance!

A Massandra Winery Winetaster

We were taken to a beautiful hall and told about the history with 10 glasses of wine sitting in front of each of us.

The beautifully presented individual wooden tray wine samples ready for tasting

Massandra

Most of the wine was very good and I think we bought a couple of bottles of the port. We left the winery in a very happy frame of mind to go and have lunch.

On our way, we stopped for a short time to view the iconic architectural monument of the Swallow's Nest.

The Swallow's Nest

Today, perched high on the Aurora cliff, this turreted fairy- tale structure, designed by architect A.Sherwood in 1911, has become the symbol of Crimea.

*Another view of
the Swallow's Nest*

It was built at the expense of the Baku oil magnate, Baron v. Steingel. The exotic Swallow's Nest has been the background in many films and now is a fashionable and expensive Italian restaurant.

Our lunch may have been in a large modern hotel but Soviet regime times die hard. A huge cauldron of soup appeared on a trolley with two formidable ladies who proceeded to serve 200 people individually. As you can imagine, by the time our soup arrived, it was stone cold. The rest of the meal followed in a similar way but we were not really hungry and instead enjoyed the entertainment by a talented Ukrainian folk–lore group.

Ukrainian singer entertainers

Russia's greatest playwright, Anton Chekhov, spent the last five years of his life living here at the White Dacha in Yalta.

This was just as I had imagined – a white cottage, containing a number of small rooms and with a verandah outside facing the garden where Chekhov could while away the evening chatting with friends – just like in his plays.

Photo collage – Lunchtime folk-lore entertainment

Chekhov was born in Taganrog near the Sea of Azov but his family moved to Moscow, where he studied medicine. In order to help support them, he began writing short stories for various literary journals. In 1886 a first collection of his work was published and, for some, it is his short stories rather than his great dramatic works which show him as a wonderful interpreter of human relationships.

AP Chekhov Memorial Museum
– Plan of the white dacha and garden

Chekhov Memorial Statue

Chekhov's White House -- Museum Poster

In March 1897, Chekhov suffered a major haemorrhage of the lungs and TB was diagnosed. He was told to change his lifestyle and move to a warmer climate. After his father's death in 1898, Chekhov bought a plot of land on the outskirts of Yalta and built a villa there.

Photograph of A P Chekhov   *Study Desk*

Piano – Once Played By Rachmaninov

A P Chekhov's White House entrance (1 of 7)
Visitors Included Leo Tolstoy, Feodor Chaliapin, Serge Rachmaninov and Maxim Gorky.

Town Square Chekhov Character / Story Monument

He designed the gardens and planted many trees here which are still flourishing, such as bamboo, magnolias and mulberry bushes.

He wrote the "The Three Sisters", "The Cherry Orchard", "The Seagull" and of course, the famous short story entitled "The Lady with The Little Dog" here in Yalta – there is a statue of this latter title in the town square.

He shared the house with his mother and sister and it soon became a meeting point for Russian writers and artists such as Leo Tolstoy, Maxim Gorky and Ivan Bunin. In 1901 he married an actress, Olga

Knipper, whom he had met during rehearsals for the play, "The Seagull".

Up to that point Chekhov, called "Russia's most elusive literary bachelor", had preferred passing liaisons and visits to brothels over commitment.

External views (rear and side) of the White House (Belaya Dacha)

Morning Room   *Bedroom*

However, their marital arrangements remained quite separate with Chekhov living mainly in Yalta and Olga in Moscow, pursuing her acting career. The literary legacy of this long-distance marriage is a correspondence which preserves gems of theatrical history, including complaints about Stanislavski's directing methods and Chekhov's advice to Olga about performing in his plays.

Chekhov's Study

Chekhov loved to travel and, unfortunately, while he was staying at a health spa in Badenweiler in the Black Forest in 1904, he died at the early age of 44.

The acre sized garden at the White Dacha, which he planted out.
100 rose bushes were a tribute to Pushkin

Study / Room

Ante - Room

Sideboard

Dining Room (painting enlarged below)

Painting In The Above Room

Inside the dacha, the rooms are still as they were in 1900 with photographs, documents, letters and all types of memorabilia and furniture carefully arranged in his study, bedroom, sitting room and dining room – even the leather coat he used to wear on his walks is hanging in the hall. On our way outside, I noticed the brass nameplate on the door still read - "A. P Chekhov". There was a small building at the back of the garden and I asked about the purpose of this.

I was told that this was where the cooking was done to avoid too many lingering odours and also where the servants lived. By this time, we were beginning to weary in need of a rest but our last visit was one not to be missed.

Entrance Door Nameplate

Just 2 miles from Yalta, the White Livadia Palace is set in a beautifully landscaped garden sloping down to the sea. This was the summer residence of Tsar Nicholas II and his family and it was here that the Yalta Conference took place in early 1945 between the leaders of the Allies, where the final defeat of

Hitler was planned by Stalin, Roosevelt and Churchill, as well as the carve-up of post-war Europe.

The 116 Room Livadia Palace

The Livadia Palace – Front Façade

The land and vineyards belonged to Count Pototsky and this was bought in 1861 by Alexander II in order to build a palace for his wife who was in poor health. The main building, the White Palace, was designed by a Russian architect named Krasnov (the same as the Cathedral) for Nicholas II and completed in 1911.

Approach to the front entrance

The main entrance portico

Entrance door detail

The design is early Italian Renaissance, of Florentine inspiration, with two very interesting interior courtyards and owes much of its marble carving to Italian craftsmen. This workmanship can be seen at the main entrance portico.

Entrance arches

Medallion initial inscriptions of each of the Emperor's Family
Inscribed at the base of each arch

The medallions over the columns still bear the initials of each of the members of the last emperor's family, by some miracle, as much was destroyed by the revolutionaries. Most people miss this important feature in their eagerness to get inside. The ground floor is given over to the venues associated with the Yalta Conference while the second floor helps to gain an insight into the lives of the last Russian royal family.

The Vestibule – (The first front hall) with the main meeting
White Hall area seen adjoining to the rear

The Vestibule, the first entrance hall, displays the basic architectural style of the palace but the "furniture cram", characteristic of interiors at that time, has disappeared gradually since nationalisation.

Now the vestibule presents the reconstruction of the furnishings of the Yalta Conference with the exception that the plenary sessions actually took place in the White Hall adjoining, but this is used for all types of International meetings to this day.

The White Hall is the most beautiful and largest room in the palace. The splendour of the stucco ceiling is accentuated by the original lighting system – almost 300 lamps are hidden behind the cornicing. During the reign of Nicholas II, the hall was used for grand receptions, banquets and balls, including the celebration of Princess Olga's 16th birthday – she was the Tsar's eldest daughter.

We then toured the various state rooms. The first was the State Recep-

The White Hall where the meetings were held

tion with walnut wainscots and ceiling, crowned with a masterpiece of a chandelier in Venetian Murano glass.

During the Yalta Conference secret talks on the Far East were held in this room, which was then President Roosevelt's study.

Prime Minister Churchill believed all the rooms were bugged and that is why he stayed at the Alupka Palace but Roosevelt was a very sick man, at the time, and could not stand the travelling.

The State Reception Room (Roosevelt's Study During the Yalta Conference)

Murano Island (Italian) Chandelier

Marshall Joseph Stalin and President Franklin D Roosevelt

The State Study of Nicholas II served as the bedroom of President Roosevelt and this is the room which has changed most, the fireplace being one of the few original features left.

The English Billiard Room (In Tudor Style) where the Yalta Documents were signed.

103

The Billiard Room, decorated in Tudor style has preserved its chestnut wainscot and a fireplace ornamented with the Emperor's initials.

All the fireplaces in the Palace are decorative, for the most part, as there was also a modern and effective system of water heating. On February 11th 1945, the resulting documents for the Yalta Conference were signed in this room.

The well-known photograph of the Big Three was taken nearby in the Italian courtyard. This feature was an indisputable success of the architect and the only change is a fountain instead of a well and ever-greens in place of roses.

Informal Time

There is another courtyard, the Arabian, but it was not meant for walks and only provided light and ventilation, but has some attractive tiles.

The Italian Courtyard

Photograph of the Big Three
The Italian Courtyard columns can be seen to the rear of the photo.

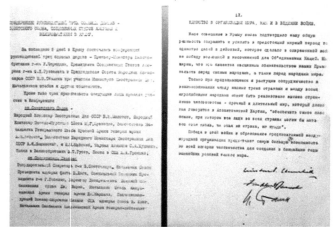

The Signed Yalta Document

A Museum Poster

From here we mounted the marble staircase to the first floor where the corridors are covered with photographs of parts of the Crimea which the royal family had visited. In the past, on this floor, were the private apartments of the Emperor, the Empress and their children, all finished in Art Nouveau style.

In a corner room with a bay window was the Study of the Tsar. The necessity of the study was quite justified as the Tsar had no private secretary and here he read documents regularly sent from the city, and here he received Ministers with their reports.

The bed chamber of the royal couple has changed beyond all recognition and this is for the better to dispel the idle and morbid curiosity of some visitors. It is an undisputable truth, despite the tragic end, that this was a happy family.

Nicholas II's Private study

Tsar's Study - Fire Place

Tsar's Study - Wall Hanging

The Tsar's Desk

Even non royalists admitted that Nicholas was an ideal family man and Alexandra an excellent mother. It was one of the rare occasions when the matrimony of the crowned persons was a love-match and not a marriage contracted solely for political reasons.

There were four daughters in the family – "a big pair" (Olga and Tatiana) and a "small pair" (Maria and Anastasia) – and the long awaited son, Alexei, whose illness (haemophilia) prematurely aged the Tsarina.

The Royal Bedchamber

The Royal Family

On the walls and on cabinets are many photographs of the children taken at different times. The family dining room is one of the cosiest rooms in the palace. Only close members of the family, Court Ministers and sometimes officers of the Imperial Yacht Standard were ever invited to dine here.

Upstairs Corridor

In fine weather, picnics and tea parties were often held out of doors.

One of the most poignant areas was the children's classroom. This was a most modest room, not out of economy, but as an element of their upbringing. The special closeness of the tutors to the family is confirmed by the fact that P.Gillard and C.Gibbs, teachers of the French and English languages, voluntarily left with their pupils for Siberia. The architect, Krasnov, gave the children lessons in painting studies and water colours by Olga and Tatiana are displayed in the room. The family used to visit in Spring and Autumn and the last occasion the Tsar was here, he went to Sevastopol to launch a ship – unfortunately it exploded in 1917.

When the revolution came and the Tsar abdicated, he requested that the family be allowed to live at Livadia but the request was refused and they were sent, first to Tobolsk, and then finally to Ekaterinburg where they were all eventually executed.

Thereafter Livadia was converted to a sanatorium and then Stalin lived there for a short time and eventually in the 1970's, it became a museum.

We returned quite tired, after a very busy day, just in time to hear the lecture on the port of Constanza, Romania but could not cope with a lecture on the Royal Engineers as our heads were packed full of information – I loved every minute. After dinner, we went straight to bed – not able for the show. (I don't think we missed much!)

Wednesday 8ᵗʰ October

Sevastopol Ukraine (Note 3)

We woke up and pulled back the curtains to find that we were in the harbour of Sevastopol surrounded by Russian and Ukrainian warships. Graham was in his element out taking photographs to left and right.

The short overnight sailing from Yalta to Sevastopol

MV Discovery berthed adjacent to naval vessels

Sevastopol cruise ship terminal

Sevastopol is a very important and historical port on the Black Sea. Founded in 1783 as a naval fortress and the base of the Black Sea Navy Fleet, it became a firm stronghold in the south of the Russian Empire. It was besieged by the British and French during the Crimean War for about a year and the city was completely destroyed afterwards.

In the 20th century, it was the home port of the Soviet Navy's Black Sea Fleet, and the city retains a significant Russian naval presence. The population is still largely ethnically Russian and the population's sympathies still lie with Moscow rather than Kiev. Russian politicians have suggested Crimea and, specifically Sevastopol, should join the Russian Federation. (Note 3)

While peaceful and stable at the moment, the political orientation towards Moscow still defines Crimea and, particularly, Sevastopol.

According to the 1997 Treaty, the Russian Naval Base is declared to be "located" in Sevastopol on the terms of a twenty year renewable lease, as I have mentioned previously.

At first, Moscow refused to recognise Ukrainian sovereignty over Sevastopol as well as over the surrounding Crimean oblast, arguing that the city was never practically integrated into the Ukrainian Soviet Socialist Republic due to its military base status.

The ex-Soviet Black Sea Fleet with all its facilities was divided between Russia's Black Sea Fleet and the Ukrainian Navy, after a continuous and sometimes violent struggle.

Our guide explained how difficult it was for her, personally, as her father was in the Russian Navy and her son was in the Ukrainian Fleet.

The two navies now co-use the city's harbours and piers but a judicial row continues over the naval base hydro-graphic infrastructure, both in Sevastopol and on the Crimean coast (especially lighthouses, historically maintained by the Soviet / Russian Navy and also used for civil navigation support).

The status of the Black Sea Fleet has a strong influence over the city's business and cultural life as the Russian society and some government representatives have never accepted the loss of Sevastopol, and tend to regard it as only temporarily separated from the homeland.

You have to remember that Sevastopol was a closed city during Soviet times and very few of the residents have any knowledge of the English language and are not accustomed to the influx of tourists as yet.

They are not impressed with foreigners who have no appreciation or understanding of their language or culture but, on the other hand, if you have bothered to learn a little of the language, even just the mastery of the Cyrillic alphabet, they will try their best to communicate with you.

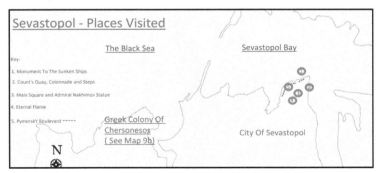

Sevastopol - Location Plan - Places Visited

Many of the passengers on our ship were on this cruise to visit the sites of the Crimean War and we had our specialist war historian on board. I found his lecture on the Crimean war very interesting but we decided to visit the city and its ancient history at the site of Chersonesos.

However, the history of the Crimean war is connected with so many of the monuments in Sevastopol that I thought I would give some outline information on the causes and results of this dreadful war.

The Crimean War (October 1854 – February 1856) was fought between the Russian Empire on one side and an alliance of the British Empire, France, the Ottoman Empire and the Kingdom of Sardinia on the other.

Most of the conflict took place on the Crimean Peninsula, but there were smaller campaigns in Western Turkey, the Baltic Sea, the Pacific Ocean and the White Sea. The war has gone by different names. In Russia it is also known as the "Oriental War" and in Britain it was sometimes called the "Russian War".

The chain of events leading to France and Britain declaring war on Russia in 1854, can be traced to the coup d'état of 1851 in France. Napoleon III sent his ambassador to the Ottoman Empire, in Turkey, to attempt to force the Ottomans to recognise France as the "sovereign authority" in the Holy Land.

Russia disputed this newest change in "authority" in the Holy Land. Pointing to two earlier treaties in the 18th century, the Ottomans then reversed their earlier decision, renouncing the French treaty and insisting that Russia was the protector of the Orthodox Christians in the Ottoman Empire.

Napoleon III responded with a show of force, sending a ship to the Black Sea - a violation of the London Straits Convention. France's show of force, combined with aggressive diplomacy and money, induced the Sultan, Abdulmecid I, to accept a new treaty, confirming France and the Roman Catholic Church as the supreme Christian authority in the Holy Land, with control over the Christian holy places and possession of the keys to the church of the Nativity, previously held by the Russian Orthodox Church.

As the conflict loomed over the question of the holy places, Nicholas I and Karl Nesselrode, the Russian-German diplomat began a diplomatic offensive which they hoped would prevent either Britain or France interfering in any conflict between Russia and the Ottomans, as well as to prevent their allying together.

The Tsar sent Prince Menshikov to Constantinople to negotiate a new treaty and at the same time Prime Minister Lord Aberdeen sent Lord Stratford to convince the Sultan to reject the treaty. Benjamin Disraeli blamed Aberdeen and Stratford's actions for making war inevitable, thus starting the process by which Aberdeen would be forced to resign because of his role in starting the war.

When the Tsar heard of the failure of Menshikov, he marched his armies into Moldavia and Wallachia, provinces on the Danube under Ottoman suzerainty, using the Sultan's failure to resolve the issue of the holy places as a pretext. Hoping to maintain the Ottoman Empire as a bulwark against the expansion of Russian power in Asia, Britain sent a fleet to the Dardanelles where it was joined by a French fleet.

However, the four great powers – Britain, France, Austria and Prussia – still hoped to find a diplomatic solution. They met in Vienna and drafted a note which they thought would be acceptable to both Russia and the Ottomans.

It was accepted in Russia but refused in Turkey following which they tried amendments to mollify the Sultan but these negotiations were fruitless.

The Sultan formally declared war on the 23rd October 1853 and proceeded to attack in the Danube region and over at the Caucasus where they were supported by Chechen Muslims.

The Battle of Sinop was the result and the subsequent destruction of the Ottoman fleet. This provided Britain and France with the "cassus belli" ie sufficient provocation for declaring war against Russia, on the side of the Ottoman Empire. Determined to address the Eastern question, the allies proposed several conditions for a peaceful resolution but the Tsar refused to comply with these and the Crimean War commenced.

The allied forces were at first mustered at the port of Varna but in August they were transported to the Crimea under the command of Lord Raglan. The army was ill-prepared, a lot of the supplies had been destroyed while troops were sitting around and waiting. There were also severe outbreaks of cholera, dysentery and insect infestation.

During the following month, allied troops landed in the Crimea and besieged the city of Sevastopol, home of the Tsar's Black Sea Fleet. The Russians had to scuttle a huge number of their ships and use the naval cannons as additional artillery and the ship's crews as marines.

Following the Battle of Balaklava, a long winter of siege warfare ensued. The Allies bombarded the city during the day and the Russians built it up again during the night. There were huge losses on both sides, aggravated by the lack of fuel, clothing and supplies.

Many of the ships carrying these items went down in storms on the Black Sea in the winter months. While the siege continued, there were campaigns taking place elsewhere, such as in the Sea of Azov where the Allies tried to undermine Russian communications and supplies to the besieged Sevastopol.

From the beginning, the Baltic campaign was a stalemate as the outnumbered Russian Baltic Fleet confined its movements to the areas around its fortifications and all the Allies could do was blockade Russian trade.

In Autumn 1854, a squadron of 3 British warships left the Baltic for the White Sea in the far northwest of Russia , where they shelled Kola (which was utterly destroyed) and Solovki but their attempt to storm Arkhangelsk proved abortive. Away over in the Pacific, a British and French Allied squadron besieged a smaller Russian force on the Kamchatka Peninsula.

An allied force was beaten back with heavy casualties in September 1854, and the Allies withdrew. The Russians escaped under the cover of snow in early 1855 when reinforcements arrived.

Even the Italians were involved as, Camillo di Cavour, under orders by Victor Emmanuel II of the Kingdom of Sardinia, sent troops to side with the British and French forces during the war. This was an attempt at gaining the favour of the French especially when the issue of uniting Italy under the Sardinian throne would become an important matter. The deployment of Sardinian troops to the Crimea allowed it to be represented at the peace conference at the end of the war, where it could address the issue of the "Risorgimento", ie Italian Unification, to other European powers.

Public opinion in Britain was very critical of the war after reading eye-witness reports in "The Times", sent back by Irishman W.H.Russell, the first journalist in history to write as a war correspondent, using the electric telegraph.

On the Russian side, Leo Tolstoy wrote "The Sevastopol Sketches", stories detailing the lives of the Russian soldiers and citizens in Sevastopol during the siege and because of this work, he was called the first war correspondent also.

Sevastopol fell on September 8th 1855. By that time the Russians, with a new Emperor, Alexander II, were already seeking peace through the Congress of Paris where the Tsar and the Sultan agreed not to establish any naval or military arsenal on the Black Sea coast.

The Treaty of Paris stood until 1871 but, with great changes in Europe :-
- the deposing of Napoleon III,
- the formation of a German State and
- further Russian interference with the Ottoman Empire,

the balance of power was altered. Encouraged by the decision of the French, and supported by the German minister Otto von Bismarck, Russia denounced the Black Sea clauses of the treaty, agreed in1856, and once again established a fleet in the Black Sea.

Notwithstanding the guarantees to preserve Ottoman territories specified in the Treaty of Paris, Russia exploited nationalist unrest in the Ottoman states in the Balkans, and seeking to regain lost prestige, once again declared war on the Ottoman Empire in 1877. In this later Russo-Turkish war, the states of Bulgaria, Romania, Serbia and Montenegro achieved independence.

Out of the 18,000 fatalities only 2,000 fell in actual battle on the British side. The Crimean war is notorious for the logistical and tactical mistakes on both sides. Nonetheless, the war is sometimes considered to be the first "modern" conflict as it "introduced technical changes which affected the future course of warfare". It highlighted the work of women who served as army nurses.

War correspondents for newspapers reported the scandalous treatment of wounded soldiers in the desperate winter conditions and prompted the work of Florence Nightingale, Mary Seacole, Frances Taylor and others and led to the introduction of modern nursing methods.

The Crimean War also saw the first tactical use of railways and other modern inventions such as the electric telegraph with the first "live" war reporting. Newspaper readership informed public opinion in Britain and France as never before and it was the first European war to be photographed.

The army system of sale of commissions came under great scrutiny, especially in connection with the Battle of Balaklava, which saw the ill-fated Charge of the Light Brigade and eventually this led to the abolition of sales of commissions.

The Crimean War was also a contributing factor in the Russian abolition of serfdom in 1861. Alexander II saw the military defeat of the Russian Serf Army by free troops from Britain and France as proof of the need for emancipation.

It equally led to the realisation by the Russian government of its current technological inferiority, namely in its military practices as well as its military weapons. The war led to the establishment of the Victoria Cross in 1856 for survivors, the British Army's first universal award for valour.

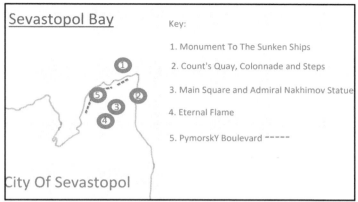

Sevastopol Walk – Places Visited

After disembarking, we walked to the Grafskaya Pristan (Count's Quay), the private landing stage of Admiral Voinovich, Commander –in-Chief of the Black Sea Fleet.

Arriving at the Grafskaya Pristan (The Count's Quay)

A wide flight of steps curves up through an antique-style colon-naded gate built in 1846, taking us directly into the city centre. In the main square stands the monument to Admiral Nakhimov, the most prominent fleet admiral of the Crimean War, who defeated the Turkish fleet and masterminded the defence of Sevastopol.

Sailors transferring from one naval building to another

View of the Grafskaya Pristan (The Count's Quay) from the Sevastopol Bay looking inland

The Grafskaya Pristan (The Count's Quay) view towards
Sevastopol Bay and beyond into the Black Sea

He suffered a fatal bullet wound to the head and died on 30th June, 1855, only a couple of months before the end of the war. The statue used to face out to the sea but the townspeople had it turned round to face the city. Facing the monument is a plaque and eternal flame honouring the soldiers who died in the Crimean and World War II. Young cadets in naval uniform stand guard in front of the monument.

From here we walked along the Primorski Boulevard, the favourite meeting place of Sevastopol citizens.

The view from here of the wide bay and the city district on the opposite side is excellent. Just off the quayside lies one of the most famous monuments in Sevastopol – it was an image of the State Emblem of the city in Soviet times.

A column, 15 metres high, stands in the water, with a bronze eagle perched on top, holding a laurel wreath in its beak. The Monument to the Scuttled Ships marks the site where Russian troops sank part of their own fleet during the Crimean War to prevent their enemies from entering the harbour.

The Monument to the Scuttled Ships

The city centre is characterised by numerous neo-classical, colonnaded buildings, typical of the Stalinist years. It is also full of Soviet memorials including a huge statue of Lenin, which we would see later on, as Sevastopol is one of the thirteen Hero Cities of the Great Patriotic War (World War II).

Sevastopol – Russian Naval Buildings including Moscow House
(Notice the St Andrews Cross flag, The Ensign of the Russian Navy reintroduced in 1992)

Sevastopol - Lenin Statue

The Greek city of Chersonesos is located about three kilometres from Sevastopol. In 1996, its open-air museum was listed as a World Heritage site by UNESCO – it has been nicknamed the "Ukrainian Pompeii" and the "Russian Troy".

Location Map - Chersonesos

Chersonesos in Greek simply means "peninsula", and aptly describes the site on which the colony was established. Apart from the beautiful location between two bays, the site is of great interest for the traces it reveals of a city with an eventful 2,000 year history.

Black Sea view from Chersonesos

Settled by Greeks in the 6th or 5th century BC, Chersonesos quickly developed into an important commercial city with 20,000 inhabitants. In the 1st century BC, it was subject to Rome until 370 AD when it was captured by the Huns. Later, during the early middle ages it became a Byzantine possession although Byzantine rule was very slight. There was a small garrison but it was more for the town's protection than for its control. It was useful to Byzantium in two ways: as an observation point to watch the barbarian tribes, and its isolation made it an ideal place of exile for those who angered the Roman and later Byzantine government.

Various popes and even the deposed Emperor Justinian II were sent here in banishment. It remained in Byzantine hands until 980AD when it reportedly fell to Kiev. Vladimir the Great agreed to evacuate the fortress only if Basil II's sister, Anna Porphyrogeneta would be given to him in marriage. The demand caused a scandal in Constantinople (Byzantium), as imperial princesses had never been married to non-Greeks before.

As a pre-condition of the marriage settlement, Vladimir was baptised here in 988AD, thus paving the way for the beginning of the Russian Orthodox Church.

After the 4th Crusade, Chersonesos became dependent on the Empire of Trebizond (Trabzon) and then fell under Genoese control in the 13th century. In 1299AD the town was sacked by the armies of the Khans and a century later it was completely destroyed and abandoned.

Chersonesos - The Amphitheatre

When the Crimea was incorporated into the Russian Empire in 1783, the new port city of Sevastopol fortunately left the old settlement area untouched, preserving it for posterity.

Chersonesos - Excavated Areas

In 1822, Russian archaeologists began excavating and discovered superimposed layers from several cultures, which enabled them to piece together the history of the town. The city wall is still in good condition and you can easily make out the rows of seats in an amphitheatre. The buildings are a great mix of Greek, Roman and Byzantine architecture including a mint for copper and silver and a large main square.

Chersonesos - Current Excavation

The Chersonesites had laid the foundation of this square during the initial planning of the city and it continued to be the central square even when the city expanded. Considering the archaeological finds in this area, it can be assumed that statues of deities, inscriptions, decrees, altars and temples were situated here in antiquity.

Perhaps the most important monument of Chersonesos, the inscribed oath, taken by young men when they came of age, was excavated here in the main square. The oath supplies evidence regarding the Chersonesos regime, where the Council and the People's Assembly were the principle bodies of government. It mentions not only the usual triad of deities (Zeus, Gaia and Helios) but also the goddess Parthenos, the great protector of the city and the state.

This oath was most probably introduced after an acute political struggle and restoration of democracy that had been temporarily lost. That was why the citizens had sworn to protect their democratic system from any infringement, to struggle against treasons, to serve the people faithfully, and to defend the frontiers from both Hellenes and Barbarians.

Chersonesos - Ruins of the Old Basilica - With St Vladimir's Cathedral in the background

Down by the shore are the ruins of a fortress, Roman baths, the columns of an 11th century basilica, with some well-preserved mosaics as well as the homes and streets of an apparently thriving community.

The largest part of the site is "the Chora", a territory of several square kilometres of now barren farmland, with the remains of wine presses and defensive towers. According to the archaeologists, the evidence suggests that the locals were paid to do the farm work, instead of being enslaved. Particular features of the city are the small fish reservoirs dotted around.

With the advent of Christianity, all cult buildings of the ancient period were either renovated or destroyed and consequently the square acquired a new outer appearance in the 9th and 10th centuries.

Up to 15 churches were discovered on the site but only partial remains of two can be seen today. During the Soviet era, the excavation site was a military area and closed off to visitors. This did not prevent, however, the plundering by the Black Sea Fleet and the local city dwellers. Still, today, tombs are pillaged.

Chersonesos - Reconstructed doorway stonework and the The Foggy Bell

Before we leave the site to visit St.Vladimir's Cathedral on the hill, I must mention the "Foggy Bell". Pictures of this bell decorate numerous books and pamphlets about Chersonesos, although it is completely unrelated to the city. In 1783, Emperor Alexander I ordered the bell to be transported to Sevastopol to be fitted in the Church of St.Nicholas which was being constructed there. After the Crimean War, the allied armies of Britain and France removed 13 church bells from Sevastopol together with other war booty. Many years later a bell with a Russian inscription was found in Notre-Dame de Paris and nobody knew how it had appeared there.

Thanks to certain diplomatic efforts on both sides, the bell was returned to the belfry of the Monastery of Chersonesos from where it was presumably taken.

The Foggy Bell and the St Vladimir Cathedral

The monastery was closed in 1925 by the new authorities, and two years later all its bells were sent away to be recast as weapons. Only one bell escaped this sad fate because the Department of the Security of Navigation of the Black and Azov Seas proposed to place it on the coast as a signal bell. Its distinct and deep peal was meant to sound the signal to passing ships in foggy weather.

Chersonesos - The Medieval Hall section of the Museum

A small museum, displaying weapons, coins, jewellery, drinking and cooking vessels etc., was located in parts of the old monastery.

We now went to admire the exterior of the Byzantine -style St Vladimir Cathedral. This church was built in the mid 19th century to honour Kiev's Grand Duke Vladimir who, according to the Rus Chronicle, was baptised here in 988.

Chersonesos - Two Views of St. Vladimir's Cathedral

The architects of the church designed a two -storey building, with a chapel on each floor.

The remains of the cruciform church where Vladimir was supposed to have been baptised are preserved on the ground floor of the modern church and are revered as the beginning of the Russian Orthodox Church.

Unfortunately the church was destroyed in the war years of 1941-1945 and now is under restoration.

Chersonesos - St. Vladimir's Cathedral - Byzantin-style design details

After enjoying the beautiful views of Artilleriyskaya Bay from Vladimir Hill, we now stopped for a short visit to another church also called St Vladimir, this time in Sevastopol itself and which is the burial place of many renowned Russian Admirals.

*Sevastopol - St Vladimir Church, Memorial to
the Heroes of the Siege Of Sevastopol (1854-1855)*

Our last stop was to see the gigantic statue of Lenin, with four corners, representing the Army, the Air Force, the Worker and the Farmer.

Reverse View - Lenin Statue overlooking the Sevastopol Bay

We enjoyed an early dinner as we had decided to take the opportunity to go to the Concert given by the Black Sea Fleet Ensemble, a former branch of the Soviet Navy, held in the Navy Officers Club.

This presented a colourful and exciting performance of Cossack dances and rousing songs but the star of the show was a balalaika player who gave a brilliant and memorable performance. Another interesting and busy day!

Thursday 9ᵗʰ October
Odessa – Ukraine

Overnight Sailing

Today we were to visit one of the most memorable cities in Ukraine – the beautiful city of Odessa. From its origin as a Greek colony established some 1,700 years ago, Odessa has grown to become one of the largest cities on the Black Sea. Numerous monuments of antiquity confirm links between this territory and the Mediterranean. In the middle ages, this area was part of Kievan Rus, the Golden Horde, the Grand Duchy of Lithuania, the Crimean Khanate and the Ottoman Empire.

In the course of the Russo-Turkish wars, it was captured by Russia at the end of the 18ᵗʰ century. Built at the behest of Catherine the Great, Odessa has had its heyday as a brilliant cultural centre and in the 19ᵗʰ century it was the fourth city of Imperial Russia after Moscow, St. Petersburg and Warsaw.

Odessa Pushkin Museum (Note 4) Statue Of The Poet Alexander Pushkin

Its historical architecture has a flavour more Mediterranean than Russian, having been heavily influenced by French and Italian styles. Odessa has always possessed a spirit of freedom and ironic humour, probably by virtue of its location and its willingness to accept and tolerate people of many different backgrounds. A wide choice of opera, ballet, concerts and plays took place every evening and many famous writers and musicians resided here.

Alexander Pushkin, one of the greatest Russian poets and writers was exiled here because of his anti-government articles; Maxim Gorky came here as a port worker in 1896; and Gogol worked on" Dead Souls" here – to name but a few.

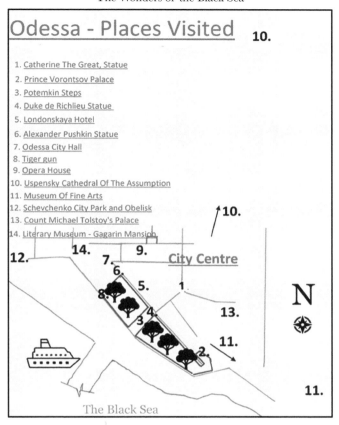

The City of Odessa - Location Map – Places Visited

It was not just the famous who were attracted by Odessa's delights as huge ethnic populations also came here from Ukrainian Russians to Greeks, Albanians, Bulgarians and Jews, and never left again.

As a free port under the Tsars, it stood open to the ideas and influences of the West but when it was threatened by invaders, who prized its strategic position, the citizens of Odessa rose fiercely to its defence.

In 1854, during the Crimean War, the city was bombarded by the Anglo-French fleet for 12 hours, but it was successfully defended and grew to be Russia's biggest port in 1881.

It was in Odessa, however, that the first stirrings of revolution were felt. In 1905 the workers rebelled and were assisted by the crew of the Russian battleship Potemkin.

There was a plan for all ships to create a simultaneous uprising later in the Autumn of 1905 but while the pre-dreadnought ship was away on exercises, rebellion broke out spontaneously.

It was sparked by the second-in-command of the battleship, who allegedly threatened reprisals against a number of the crew for their refusal to eat rotten meat. Reportedly, he mustered the crew on the quarterdeck near where a tarpaulin was laid out and armed marines were drawn up.

The sailors assumed that a group execution was pending and rushed at the marines (themselves sailors) calling on them not to shoot.

The actual events sparking off the mutiny remain uncertain and have been overshadowed by the version presented in the famous Sergei Eisenstein film "The Battleship Potemkin".

Certainly, discipline in the Russian Navy was harsh and morale was very low after so many defeats in the Russo-Japanese Wars. The uprising was suppressed in Odessa and pogroms began causing 13% of the population (many of them Jews) to flee the city.

Pogroms are organized persecution and extermination of an ethnic group coming from the Russian word for destruction.

During the Bolshevik Revolution, Odessa suffered greatly and changed hands several times, including the Ukrainian Tsentral'na Rada, the French Army, the Red Army and the White Army. After the Revolution, Ukraine enjoyed a brief period of independence but despite Lenin's promises, the Red Army invaded and, by 1920, most of Ukraine was Bolshevik ruled.

Joseph Stalin, fearing Ukrainian nationalism, killed the intelligentsia, and, through his policy of collectivization, engineered a famine in 1932 and 1933 that took at least 5 million lives.

During World War II, Odessa endured a 73day siege by German troops and in 1941 the citizens were eventually overcome, with the resistance moving underground to the catacombs.

Nazi occupation scourged the country and the city suffered severe damage and many casualties —approximately 60,000 Odessans (mainly Jews) were either massacred or sent to labour or concentration camps.

After this war, Soviet rule prevailed – it was one of the first four Soviet cities to be awarded the title of "Hero City" in 1945.

A political meltdown occurred in December 1991, when 90% of Ukrainians voted for independence, in effect dissolving the Soviet Union. However, Ukraine faces ongoing border disputes with Russia to this day.(Note 3)

Odessa - Catherine the Great Statue, Ekaterinskaya Square

Our morning began by walking to Ekaterinskaya Square with its huge statue of Catherine the Great – I think this is a recent addition - where we had to step, carefully over the sand and cement as the whole square was being re-paved.

Just to the north west of this square stands Prince Vorontsov's Palace, a name you will recognise from Yalta, where his summer residence, the Alupka Palace was built. After its destruction in World War II, this mansion was built in a faithful reconstruction of the original classical revival style (1826-27) by Boffo.

Mikhail Vorontsov, as I mentioned in Yalta, was the energetic and dynamic Governor-General of Novo-Russia and Odessa's first administrator.

Odessa was a burgeoning new trade centre with a population which doubled between 1823 and 1849, in spite of two outbreaks of bubonic plague and two cholera epidemics during this period.

Odessa Architecture - City centre buildings

A 19th century commentator wrote....

"Odessa in the 1830's combined all that was cultured, rich and refined in Russian society and which for one reason or another did not sit well with life in the capital or abroad. The southern climate, the warmth and sunshine for most of the year, the wonderful, gleaming rainbow-hued Black Sea ... the Italian opera ... the resonant Italian voices in the streets, the cheapness of the free seaport, and generally just the freedom and ease of life in this half-foreign, half-Russian town, together with the enlightened and accessible nature of its Governor, Vorontsov, inspired the warmest feelings for Odessa."

Challenges also came of a personally painful kind. The dissident poet, Alexander Pushkin, who worked in the Foreign Office, was sent to Odessa to put him at a safe distance from St. Petersburg after he was suspected, correctly, of anti-state activities.

Soon after Vorontsov's appointment as Governor-General, Pushkin began a love affair with his wife, Countess Vorontsova.

Scandal travelled quickly in Odessa and, not surprisingly, the two men did not get on.

Pushkin famously described Vorontsov as " half-milord, half merchant", probably because of his long association with Britain but not an entirely fair description of a man who had distinguished himself so much on the battlefield.

Vorontsov responded to the situation by using his position to have Pushkin appointed to a travelling commission to study locust damage in the Dniester Region. Pushkin went under protest but reportedly did no work of any value as he was writing "Eugene Onegin" at the time.

Odessa - Alexander Pushkin Statue, City Hall   *Odessa - City centre direction sign*

By 1824, Vorontsov had reached the end of his tether and, through friends in St. Petersburg, secured Pushkin's dismissal from the Foreign Service.

This meant that Pushkin had to leave Odessa, ending his affair with the Countess although, apparently, he wore the gold talisman ring she had given him until the day he died in a duel thirteen years later.

*Odessa-Potemkin steps–View down from the top Odessa-Potemkin steps
View up seen from sea Level*

From the square we walked on to the top of the famous Potemkin Steps of cinematographic fame. Originally known as the Maritime Stairs, the steps were built in 1837-1842 by the Italian architect F.K. Boffo.

The 192 steps create an optical illusion – from below you can only see steps while from above you can only see landings and although they appear to be built on parallel lines, they are nearly twice as wide at the bottom as at the top.

The legendary staircase is one of the most famous scenes in motion picture history.

In Eisenstein's film 'The Battleship Potemkin', produced to commemorate the uprising, a most famous scene is included where hundreds of Odessans are murdered on the steps, culminating in the haunting scene of a baby carriage that bounces down nearly all the monumental 192 steps to the sea.

The actual massacre took place in the streets nearby, not on the steps themselves, but the film has caused many to visit Odessa to see the site of the "slaughter".

Odessa Statue - Duke De Richelieu - Standing at the top of the Potemkin Staircase

At the top of the staircase stands the statue of the Duke de Richelieu, clad in a toga and facing the sea front, built by Russian sculptor Martos in 1826.

In 1801, Armand du Plessis, Duc de Richelieu, was appointed the first mayor of Odessa by Tsar Alexander I. After cleaning up a corrupt administration, Richelieu transformed this Black Sea village into a flourishing city with banks, institutes and theatres - even with street lighting installed.

He constructed port facilities and encouraged agriculture and commerce but after he returned to France, Odessa suffered dreadful neglect until Vorontsov arrived.

From here, we took a leisurely walk along the Primorsky Boulevard, a wide cobblestone street with tall trees, providing scenery that rivals Paris.

Half- way along the street stands the famous Londonskaya Hotel which has spectacular views of the Black Sea.

Odessa - The Peaceful Primorsky Boulevard

This hotel opened 160 years ago and is still considered a special place to stay in Odessa. It has been a part of history with its corridors witnessing many significant guests – many different political leaders, including Margaret Thatcher, and Isadora Duncan.

Odessa - The Londonskaya Hotel Main Entrance / Frontage

At the end of the boulevard stands the statue of the Poet Alexander Pushkin, the pink and white colonnaded City Hall resembling a Greek temple, and various museums.

*Odessa - City Hall and the Alexander Pushkin Statue
at the western end of Primorski Boulevard*

Odessa- Political Demonstration in Front of the City Hall

As we approached, a sea of red flags waving, the noise of angry speeches and the high presence of policemen, made us wonder what was afoot.

Unfortunately, the precarious Ukrainian government had been dissolved the night before and this milling crowd was the old communist adherents out demanding the return of the old regime. Although watched by police, Graham was in his element photographing the assembly.

Our guide, naturally tried to play down the situation and led us nearby to see the Tiger Gun, salvaged from HMS Tiger, a British ship which sank in 1854 during the Crimea campaign.

Almost directly across from here stands the beautiful and world-renowned Odessa Opera House and Ballet Theatre, designed in the 1880's by Viennese architects Fellner and Helmer.

The Odessa Opera House – External Views

The Odessa Opera House - Main Entrance Staircase

Constructed in only three years, it blends a number of different architectural styles including Viennese, Baroque and Italian Renaissance and it is considered one of the most fascinating and important architectural masterpieces in the city .The first Opera House was opened 1810, almost on the same spot, and was called the Odessa Theatre. It was financed by the newly instituted quarantine fees of Vorontsov.

When ticket sales were low, the owner, also the Medical Officer, would announce the discovery of an infection among newly arrived passengers and ordered them quarantined at their own cost.

The expenses of the Lazaretto (a hospital for persons with infectious diseases), where passengers had stayed, would be used to hire a major performer for the theatre.

Unfortunately, the building was gutted by fire in 1873. The new theatre was completed in1887and cost 1,300,000 Roubles and it was the first building in Odessa to employ the Edison Company to install illumination.

To keep the theatre patrons comfortable in the summer, workers would lower wagonloads of ice and straw down a 35 foot shaft, then would carry it through a tunnel to a basement beneath the hall, where cool air rose up through the vents beneath the seats.

The Odessa Opera House - Main Auditorium

The theatre was burnt down again in 1925 and its latest remodelling was in 1960.Many famous singers have performed here, Caruso and Chaliapin, to name but two.

However, the theatre sits upon shifting ground and has been in danger of collapse. The first cracks in the foundation appeared almost as soon as the theatre opened and the eastern half sagged almost seven inches in its first three years, and six walls began to tilt. Gleb Dranov, a former opera singer who sang at the theatre for 25 years, and who worked as a geologist, is helping to repair the building. At the entrance are stone figures depicting scenes from Aristophanes and Euripides. There are also allegorical sculptures representing the Goddess of Tragedy, in a chariot drawn by four panthers, Orpheus, charming the centaur with his music and cherubs playing, singing and dancing. In the niches are busts of Pushkin, Gogol, Griboyedov and Glinka, representing poetry, comedy, drama and music.

Opera House Entrance Rooftop Sculpture – Chariot Drawn By Panthers

The auditorium is in the style of Louis XVI with a chandelier that weighs almost two and a half tons, surrounded on the ceiling by frescoes depicting scenes from Shakespeare's Twelfth Night, A Midsummer Night's Dream, A Winter's Tale and As You Like It. The architects, remembering the previous fires have provided the theatre with 24 exits. Unfortunately, we could not see the inside because of renovation work so this must be a return, to visit.

Odessa- Uspensky Cathedral of the Assumption

Our next call was to the magnificent Uspensky Cathedral of the Assumption. It was built in 1855-1869 in Russo Byzantine style in honour of the Assumption of the Virgin.

Boasting an ensemble of five sweeping domes and a very tall bell tower of 56 metres, this was the highest building in Odessa until after World War II. The cathedral's blue and white interior is truly impressive.

It has an upper and lower temple, holds 5,000 people and contains some priceless icons of the Russian Orthodox Church. It is one of the few cathedrals of Odessa which has survived as a cathedral throughout the Soviet era and when we visited, a service was in progress to a packed congregation.

During Nazi occupation in World War II, on the eve of the anniversary of the October Revolution, November 6, 1943, Georgi Dyubakin, a Youth Communist League member, hoisted the soviet red flag on top of the cathedral.

He inscribed "Greetings to our friends and death to our enemies" on the flag in bright white letters. Under this he wrote the warning "mined". The red flag flew over the occupied city for all of the day, bringing a brief hope to the occupied residents.

Odessa Museum of Fine Arts (The Former Prince Stanislav Pototsky Palace)

In the former Palace of Prince Stanislav Pototsky, we find the Odessa Museum of Fine Arts. The Palace which has a six- column Corinthian portico, a bas-relief frieze and lateral wings forms a deep semi-circular court. It was built between 1805-1810 in a Russian style, by an unknown architect, for the Pototsky family.

Odessa - Local arts on sale near the Museum Of Fine Arts

149

There are many stories and legends about the matriarch in this family, Sofia Pototsky. It is very difficult to find information about this lady but I have gathered together some interesting facts.

The story begins in the Turkish city of Bursa where, in 1762, Sofia was born into the family of a Greek cattle merchant. When her father died, her mother Maria, left without resources, became a courtesan.

In 1777, Maria introduced her beautiful daughter to Karol Boskamp-Liasopolski, the Polish ambassador in Istanbul – it is said that her mother sold her to this man.

Impressed by Sofia's beauty, he invited her to his Palace. There were French lessons, high society parties and trips to Warsaw. This new land changed her life forever and 39 year old Joseph de Vitt, son of Jan de Vitt, the Governor of Kamenets- Podolsk, fell ardently in love with the foreign girl.

There are still stories told of their secret wedding in the village church of Zinkivski and about Joseph's father, who was very angry and his mother, who became ill with the grief.

From Kamanets, in her status of Joseph de Vitt's wife – he was by now a General in the Russian Army – Sofia went travelling across Europe.

Unfortunately, her husband had to play second fiddle as Sofia's beauty and cleverness made her a favourite in all the courts of Europe, especially with King Friedrich II of Prussia and Austrian Emperor Joseph II.

However, fame breeds envy and gossips spread that the lady was a Russian spy and a paramour of Grigory Potemkin. Everyone felt very sorry for poor Joseph.

In October 1791, in Yassy, then capital of Moldova (now in Romania), where de Vitt was stationed, Sofia met Count Pototsky for the first time. Love disarmed the married Count and scandal and rumour spread about the couple from Vienna to St. Petersburg.

There are many legends surrounding the story that say Pototsky literally bought Sofia from her husband Joseph de Vitt.

From 1796-1805, Pototsky created, for his dear wife, a piece of her native Greece in the form of a huge park in Uman with grottoes, lakes, waterfalls, fountains, pavilions and 500 species of tree.

The building of the park cost fifteen million zloty (2 million Silver Roubles) and nearly bankrupted him. Count Pototsky was advised by the ex-husband to sell Sofia yet again and recoup his losses. The untimely death of the magnate in 1805 prevented the implementation of all his ideas.

Here the story becomes vague (some day I will find out) but I know she had 13 children and I believe either Olga or Alexander lived in this Palace.

The plaque on the front of the palace states that "This palace was donated to Odessa in 1889 by Grigori Marazili, a well- known arts patron, to build a Fine Arts Museum" – it was opened in 1899.

The original collection consisted of a small group of pictures of the Odessa drawing school and over seventy paintings donated by St. Petersburg Academy of Arts. Before the Revolution, the museum contained many canvases by Western European masters but almost no works of Ukrainian art.

Fine Arts Museum Plaque

After the Revolution, many private collections in Odessa were seized and were incorporated into the collection. Inside, the many spacious halls have painted and moulded ceiling decorations, fine marble mantelpieces and patterned parquet floors, and the 26 rooms store a wide range of fine arts – paintings, graphics, sculptures and decorative art.

There is a special room provided for the exhibition of Russian and Ukrainian icons from the 16th and 17th centuries.

Among the collection are works of the famous artists Levitsky, Ayvazovsky, Repin, Surikov and Shiskin – the names may not mean much but the paintings are easily recognisable.

There are also some early works of Kandinsky – we enjoyed the art so much that we bought a disc showing all the paintings.

At the end of the building they had set up a display of local folk art, much of which was for sale. My Russian was used to purchase a painted box much to the surprise of the craft lady in attendance.

Driving through the city, glancing at all the famous and important buildings which were pointed out for our attention, we reached the Shevchenko City Park, named after the Ukrainian poet and patriot.

The park is large with an area of 225 acres and has a wonderful view of the Black Sea – together with its own beach, a vast stadium, a theatre and observatory.

The Odessa fortress, also in the park, retains some of the original parts – the old tower and wall – of the military fortress built in 1793. The park is also home to the World War Memorial called the Alley of Glory, constructed in 1961.

*Odessa – 'The Alley Of Glory' Memorial Obelisk, Shevchenko City Park,
looking out to the Black Sea*

The obelisk with an eternal flame burns in commemoration of the Unknown Sailor, where a guard of chosen local school children is changed every fifteen minutes. A very impressive sight!

Odessa - Chosen local school children changing guard at the Eternal Flame – above and below

In the afternoon, we had opted for a trip called Noble Odessa where we were to explore the rich cultural heritage by visiting three fine estates that today house some of the city's most notable museums.

Odessa has for centuries been an inspiration to artists, poets, writers and musicians and was almost as popular as Vienna in its day.

Sviataslav Richter, the wonderful pianist, was a son of this city. We were lucky enough to see him perform in Inverness, many years ago. I remember the performance very well firstly, for the magnificence of his playing and secondly, for the fact that he never smiled once, even when taking his bow. Of course, at that time, in the 70s, he was accompanied everywhere by his KGB minders.

It was a short drive to the estate of the Russian magnate Novikov, where the former Palace is now the Museum of Local Lore and History.

The Odessa Museum of Local Lore and History   *Museum - Wall hanging and former dress*

The house was built in 1876, according to the plans of F.Gonsiorivsky, who blended the architecture of revolutionary concepts of 19th century advanced design with various classical styles.

Museum Interior

The first exhibition, opened in August 1944, was "Odessa Heroic Defence", dedicated to the resistance of Odessa citizens to the Nazis during WWII. The actual Local Lore and History Museum was opened on May 6th, 1956.

Here we saw the history of the development and growth of Odessa from the first days of settlement in the area until modern day life in the city.

Documents, decorative arts, numismatic collections and weapons, all part of the History and Antiquities Society of Odessa, were on display. It helped to put all the information we had received in the morning into some sort of order and with a better understanding.

We then continued on to the estate of Count Mikhail Tolstoy, which houses the Scientists' Club of Odessa.

The palace began as a one-storey home for Count Tolstoy, a distant cousin of Leo Tolstoy, the celebrated writer, but in 1897, the Opera House architects, Fellner and Helmer, designed a two-storey addition with façades copying the style of Italian Baroque.

Next to the building is a beautiful landscaped garden, encircled by a cast iron railing, which was designed by F. Duphen in the 1880's. The triple-flight staircase of marble led us to the White Hall with a large rotunda.

Michael Tolstoy Building – Scientists' Club of Odessa

The building was restored in 1975 and the 33 halls (we did not see all of them) are rich in decoration and very elegant.

Since 1932, part of the building has been used as the Scientists' Club of Odessa. We entered this through a monumental arch, crowned with the mask of a lion to see a large lecture room, much like a theatre.

The Silk Lounge and Marble Lounge are filled with collections of photographs and furniture that once belonged to the Tolstoy family.

It was here that I saw the most beautifully painted and carved grand piano and I was allowed to try it out. Franz Liszt was a guest here and gave a recital on this piano in the evening.

Franz Liszt's Piano

Of course, he had brought his own piano but when he was leaving he decided that it was too much trouble to move again and so he left his piano in the room, where it has stood to this day.

Audrey Trying Out Franz Liszt's Grand Piano

Franz Liszt's Grand Piano – Woodwork details

The Nut-Tree Room was charming with its original furniture and rich decoration and it was here that our guide told us more about the Tolstoy family in Odessa.

Count Tolstoy, who had always been a great philanthropist and did many things for the city, had a son also called Mikhail.

This son fell in love with the family laundry maid, Helen, and he married her. In those days this was unheard of and the family were completely shunned by Odessan society.

However, Helen studied and learned the attributes of a lady and, because of her pleasant nature and many acts of charity, she was eventually accepted by the people who had once shunned her. Unfortunately, her husband died of spinal T.B. but she carried on with her many causes for the poorer people of the city.

When the revolution came, she built a hospital for the city and one would think that, because of her work and being a domestic worker in her early life, she would have been spared. Unfortunately, this was not to be the case and the revolutionaries drove Helen and her family out of their home and out of the city. Helen and her elder son died of poverty in Paris a few years later.

I love to hear these real stories of the people who lived in the building, it gives me a feeling of empathy with the rooms and the articles in them. I hoped playing Liszt's piano might have transferred some of his talent, but I don't think so!

Double Entrance Staircase (Gagarin Mansion) Literary Museum

Our last Palace was the Gagarin Mansion which, since 1977, has been home to the Literary Museum. This building was constructed in the middle of the 19th century for the nobleman Prince Gagarin, one of the first citizens of Odessa.

Each of the 20 halls is decorated in its own specific style, typical for the period of literature, to which it was dedicated. Unfortunately, we had time only to visit three rooms. The first contained a huge sail explaining the origin of the name Odessa – some thought to be from Odysseus, the Greek wanderer.

Self Portrait - The Poet,
Alexander Pushkin

Then we entered the Literary Room, which was filled with rare editions, manuscripts, photographs and albums, tracing the rich literary heritage of Odessa, connected with such names as Pushkin, Ostovsky, Bunin, Twain, Gorky and Mayakovski.

The Poet Pushkin
Memorabilia / Family Tree

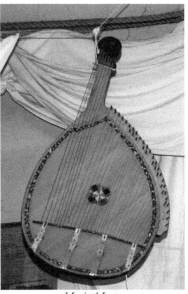

Musical Instrument
Display

The Golden Hall or Gala Hall made us gasp because of the beauty of the decoration and also the fact that we were handed a glass of champagne on entering. Franz Liszt performed here, as well, but today we were going to hear the talented students of the Stoliarsky Music School presenting a classical violin recital – excellent!

Gagarin Mansion Golden Hall - Recital Room

Odessa Stoliarsky Music School Recital

This building had also been a hotbed for revolutionaries in 1825. Meetings were held in the salon by progressive-minded Russian army officers, who attempted a coup against the autocratic government of Nicholas I – these were 'the Decembrists'. The revolt went disastrously wrong in St. Petersburg and all the people connected, even from Odessa, were rounded up and either shot or sent to Siberia in exile. The Decembrist revolt profoundly affected Russia, leading to increased police terrorism, exile in Siberia, and the spread of revolutionary societies among the young intellectuals.

They were later regarded as martyrs and founders of the 19th Century Russian Revolutionary Movement.

It was also in this hall that Vladimir (Zeev) Zhabotinski declaimed his idea for the creation of a free state of Israel.

Time To Leave Odessa

A Harbour Serenade to send us off

What an amazing day – this will definitely be on my list of favourite cities. After dinner, we listened to another classical concert (gluttons for punishment) and then off to bed.

Friday 10th October 2008

Constanza, Romania.

Overnight sailing to Constanza

Constanza - Harbour

uilt on and around a promontory of land extending into the Black Sea, Constanza has been a seaport since 6BC. The legendary Jason and the Argonauts, when they returned from their quest for the Golden Fleece, laid anchor on the site upon which Greek colonists founded the town of Tomis in 657BC.

A number of inscriptions found in this seaport and its vicinity show that Constanza is situated where the town of Tomis once stood. According to one myth, found in the Biblioteca, the town was founded by Aeetes, son of Helios, the sun God :

*"When Aeetes discovered the daring deeds done by Medea, he started off
in pursuit of the ship: but when she saw him near, Medea murdered her
brother (also his son) and cutting him limb from limb, threw the pieces
into the deep. Gathering the child's limbs, Aeetes fell behind in the pursuit: wherefore he turned back, and, having buried the rescued limbs of his
child, he called the place Tomi".*

Another legend is recorded by Jordanes, who ascribes the foundation of the city to a Getae (Goth) queen:

*"After achieving this victory (against Cyrus the Great) and winning so
much booty from her enemies, Queen Tomyris crossed over into that part
of Moesia, which is now called Lesser Scythia, and built on the Moesian
shore of the Black Sea, the city of Tomi, named after herself".*

The Black Sea is certainly the place for legend, with each country
having their own versions, but they all agree that this was definitely
the land of Jason and the Argonauts.

In 29BC, the Romans captured the region and under their influence, or more strictly their domination from the 3rd century BC
onwards, the port grew and prospered.

After the split of the Roman Empire, Tomis fell under the jurisdic-
tion of the Eastern Roman Empire.

Emperor Constantine greatly expanded the city, adding a quarter
called Constantiana, in honour of his half-sister around 237- 337 A.D.

Tomis – Constantia experienced a golden age under Justinian and,
lying at the seaward end of the Great Trajan Wall, there are many
remains which prove that it must have been surrounded by many
fortifications.

About the 6th century AD, the city fell into obscurity for a long time
and there is very little remaining evidence to find the reason for this.

Towards the end of the medieval period, Genoese merchants and
sailors revived the city, using it as a stop on their trade routes – they
gave it the name Constanza.

During those dark ages after the Roman defeat, however, the
Romanians clung to their Roman heritage and Latin-derived
language, and dreamed of independence.

After successively becoming part of the Bulgarian Empire, the independent principality of Dobrotitsa and Wallachia, Constanza fell under Ottoman rule around 1419.

As the power of the Ottomans dwindled, Russia ruled as protectorate over Moldavia and Wallachia until 1856.

The language became a symbol of Romanian aspirations, which were finally realised in the 19th century when Moldavia and Wallachia were united into one country, Romania – Transylvania became a part of Romania only after WWI.

During WWI, Romania was on the side of the Allies and Constanza became a large industrial and maritime centre.

However, in WWII Romania joined the Axis powers and was occupied by the Nazis throughout the war – Constanza was one of the main targets of the Allied bombers and suffered extensive damage.

In 1944, Romania was liberated by the Soviet army, King Michael abdicated from a royal dynasty which had existed since the 16th century, and the People's Republic of Romania was declared.

Another tragic episode of Romania's history was when Nicolae Ceausescu became President. He was deposed and executed as recently as 1989. Romania became part of the European Union in 2007.

Today Constanza, located in the Dobruja region, is the largest city in the region and has become a flourishing trade port linking the markets of land-locked countries from Central and Eastern Europe with the rest of the world.

Most of Constanza's historical attractions are in the vicinity of Ovid Square.

Constanza - Ovid Square and Archaeological Museum Signs

In AD8, the Roman poet, Ovid, was banished here by the Emperor Augustus and died here 8 years later.

The reason for his exile is believed to be his discovery of an illicit affair between the Emperor's daughter and an ordinary soldier.

He wrote some of his most important work in Tomis expressing his sadness at being so far from home in his poems "Tristria" and "Epistulae ex Ponte".

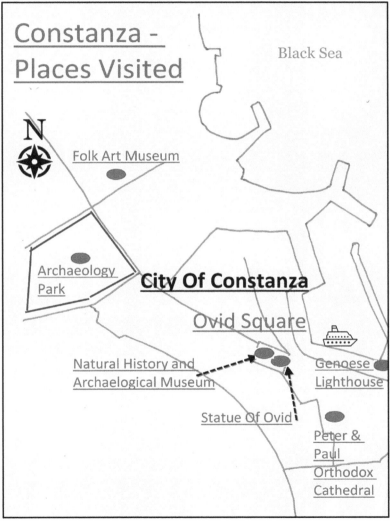

Constanza – Location Map

Ovid Statue

Tomis was by his own account "a town located in a war-stricken cultural wasteland on the remotest margins of the Empire."

A statue of Ovid, Publius Ovidius Naso, by sculptor Ettore Ferrari in 1887, stands in the main square of Constanza.

To best appreciate Constanza's long history a visit to the Archaeological Museum, housed in the old town hall, is necessary.

Constanza Archaeological Museum

The entire history of this area, the province of Dobruja, is covered, beginning with a collection of Neolithic tools and weapons.

A large section is devoted to the Dacians, a Thracian tribe who set up an extensive culture all over Romania.

Another section details the founding of the first cities on the Black Sea, Tomis, Histria and Callatis. We saw glass bottles for babies' milk and jars for collecting blood and much gold jewellery.

In the Treasure Hall we found the museum's finest pieces, including a statue of the goddess Fortuna with Pontos, god of the Black Sea and a superb Glycon, the protective god of homes and temples, in the form of a snake with a horse's head and human ears. Both works date from the 2nd and 3rd century AD.

Glass Bottle Display

Fortuna With Pontos,
God Of The Black Sea

The Glykon Serpen −Divinity Of Good, Patron Of House and Family,
Guardian Of Temples. Tomis

The Thinker and His Wife - Homonglo Idols
From Necropolis Cemovodo (5000 – 4500 BC)

A short walk from the museum brought us to the Mosaic Monument. This vast complex, only a few steps from the statue of Ovid, is on three levels, and once linked the upper town to the harbour.

The World's Largest Mosaic from this era

The enormous mosaic terrace, of which about one-third of the original 100m by 20m is still intact, is the world's largest mosaic floor still in existence from this era.

Built in the first half of the 4th century AD, this former marketplace and warehouse is now protected by a modern building – architectural remains still show the existence of shops, warehouses and workshops. As you look out from the immense floor to the old port, you can imagine the people of Tomis gathering to watch the ships docking. Nearby are the vestiges of Roman baths with remnants of a complete indoor plumbing system, central heating and ventilation and aqueducts which had brought fresh water to the city from six miles distant.

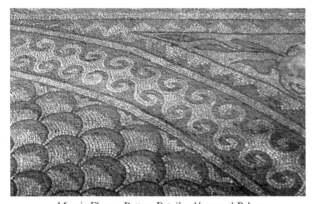

Mosaic Floor – Pattern Detail - Above and Below

With a short detour, we reached the Archaeology Park, an open-air museum along the Republican Boulevard. Here we came across columns, sarcophagi, amphoras and other remains.

Archaeology Park - Republican Boulevard of ancient stone pedestals with Funerary Inscriptions

Reverse View Of The Boulevard   *Example Stone Pedestal*

The museum also includes part of the ancient ramparts of Tomis and a tower once owned by the Brotherhood of Butchers (or so says the very old inscription).

Along this Boulevard were many inscriptions on the stone pedestals and I spent quite some time reading these and although they were written almost 2,000 years ago, the sentiments are the same as today.

I have noted one or two examples of Funerary Epigrams below...

"Hermogenes was my name, but they called me the Cyzician; I was with dignity arhontes in my homeland and fulfilled the role of an agoranamus. I considered friendship for all as a title of glory. At the age of fifty, reaching the end of life, I died, as the term must come for all. Salutation passer-by!"

- Funerary Epigram Tomis 3ʳᵈ century AD.

"Remembrance. Nothing depends on humans, everything turns under the power of destiny. Because I, myself, tried to raise a child and lead him to the fulfilment of hope. But my will was preceded by the decision (of fate) by the grave. As the decision of fate is, my cherished, I paid the destiny deserved by me before reaching the age of maturity and joining the row of men. Being a child aged 6, little and young, my name was Lilias. To whom I raised this grave, as it should not have been, I, Bassanius, his father, together with my wife, Ianuria, the too much tear shedding, mourning together the child's painless birth. Salutation passer-by and again health for the others."

- Funerary Epigram, Tomis 4ᵗʰ century AD

"Andrys built this funerary monument, carved skilfully, for his deceased wife - Kyrille, to remember her outstanding wisdom she had in marriage and in life. Devout deed was done only by the burial. Because he knows that the memory of those who were before is flourishing for the mortals remaining. (Also) he understood that time destroys everything, but retains this : the glory of the living and the virtue of those who are dead."

- Funerary Epigram Tomis 3ʳᵈ – 4ᵗʰ century AD.

"Perinthos, my husband, raised the altar and stele. And if you want to know, passer-by, who and whose I am (listen): when I was 13 a young man loved me, worthy of us; then I married him and bore three children : a son first and then two daughters. The very image of my face; finally I bore a fourth time, though I should not have any more. Because the child died first and short time after, me too. I left the light of the sun when I was thirty. I, Cecilia Artemisia lie here. Home and husband for me is Perinthos. My son's name is Priscus and my daughter's Hieronis; as regards Theodora, she was a child in the house when I died. My husband,

Perinthos, lives and mourns me with faint voice. As well, my dear father weeps because I retreated here. I also have here my mother Flavia Theodora. Here also lies my husband's father, Caecilius Priscus. I arrived in this family but behold I died. A salutation to you too whoever you should be, you who pass by our graves!"

-Funerary Epigram Tomis 2ⁿᵈ – 3ʳᵈ century AD.

" Salutation passer-by ! You stopped, saying to yourself in your mind : who and where from is this one (who lies here)? Listen stranger, my homeland and my name. My place (of origin) before, was Hellada. I was born (that means) from a mother from Athens and my father was coming from Hermione, and my name is Epiphania. I saw many lands and sailed all over the sea because my father, as well as my husband, were ship owners, whom after death, I laid in the grave, with clean hands. Really happy was my life before! I was born among muses and I shared the goods of wisdom. As a woman, to women, I gave much (help) to abandoned wives, being ruled by pious sentiments. Also I much helped the one retained on the bed by suffering. Because I well realised that mortal's fate is not according to piousness. Hermogenes, the Acyrian and Tomitan, from the Oinopes tribe, full of gratitude to his wife, devoted (this monument) as remembrance."

- Funerary Monument, 2ⁿᵈ – 3ʳᵈ century AD.

These epigrams, roughly translated from the Latin, fascinated me as the amount of early Roman social history contained in them is boundless. Also, now the deceased have been remembered once again.

I always say that everyone has two deaths: the first when the body ceases to exist and the second, the worst, when we are forgotten – the Roman citizens obviously felt the same way.

We proceeded to a more modern religious centre, that of the Peter and Paul Orthodox Cathedral. Although this area was ruled for a long time by the Ottomans and there are a number of significant Mosques, other religions were tolerated. The Russians maintained authority over the Orthodox Churches.

Constanza - Peter and Paul Orthodox Church – Entrance and internal Views

Constructed in Greco - Roman style between 1883 and 1885, this church was severely damaged during WWII and was restored in 1951.The interior murals display a neo - Byzantine style combined with Romanian elements best observed in the iconostasis and pews, chandeliers and candlesticks are made of bronze and brass alloy.

These were all designed by Ion Mincu and completed in Paris. Inside the dark building, heavy with incense and candle smoke there are some wonderful marble columns and inspiring frescoes and a copper roof.

In Orthodox Churches, nobody sits down, the service is conducted with everyone standing and it was surprising to see so many women taking important parts in the service.

Constanza - Peter and Paul Orthodox Church – Decoration and Lighting

Church Relic

Apparently the priest has to be married before he is given a church and congregation to look after, as his wife plays a significant role.

While we were there, a special religious relic was being venerated and as soon as the service was over, three priests bundled up the box containing the relic, put it into the back of their old car and went off to another church to celebrate there.

Our last visit was to the Folk Art Museum where we saw a collection of pottery, paintings, icons and other domestic objects from the communities in the countryside and a superb display of costumes from different areas around.

Folk Art Museum

We were allowed some free time and taken to the only tourist shop - where the prices were astronomical - so we left for a wander around. The city is very run-down with many crumbling buildings.

Constanza - Folk Art Museum - Local costume Display

Constanza - Local Buildings

Apparently, as in Turkey, they cannot demolish derelict buildings until an owner is found and this proves impossible at times.

The people were friendly but most appeared to have a very hard life. The electricity system in the town is unbelievable. Ten or twenty cables are strung across the roads, and not very high either, and at the junctions, the tangled knots are mind − boggling and seem very unsafe - (the photographs highlight this).

The Constanza Genoese Lighthouse

As we left the busy port, we could see a huge structure on the front and enquired what this was and why it was sitting empty. This had been a sumptuous casino built between the two World Wars in art nouveau style according to the plans of architects, Renard and Antonescu.

It is a striking building with a wonderful view of the sea but it is sitting derelict. Because of the poverty in the country, a casino is not required at the moment. Leaving the harbour, the Genoese lighthouse is another reminder of Constanza's history. Soaring to a height of 26 feet, this lighthouse was built in 1860 by the Danube and Black Sea Company to honour the Genoese merchants who established a flourishing sea trade community here in the 13th century.

I cannot leave my first visit to Romania without mentioning Transylvania, that well-known region of this country and its infamous creation of Dracula. Some say that Transylvania sits on one of the earth's strongest magnetic fields and that its people have extra-sensory perceptions.

Vampires are believed to hang around crossroads on St. George's Day, April 23rd and the eve of St. Andrew, November 29th. The area is also home to Bram Stoker's Dracula. Count Dracula, a fictional character in the Dracula novel, which was inspired by one of the best known figures of Romanian history − Vlad Dracul, nicknamed Vlad Tepes (Vlad the Impaler) − was a ruler of Wallachia (1456 − 1462). Vlad Tepes was born in December 1431, in the fortress of Sighisoara, Romania. Vlad's father, governor of Transylvania, had been inducted into the Order of the Dragon about one year before.

The order could be compared to the Knights Templar or the Teutonic Order of Knights and was a semi- military and religious society, originally created in 1387 by the Holy Roman Emperor and his wife, Barbara Cilli. The main goal of a secret fraternal order of knights was to protect the rights of Christianity and to crusade against the Turks.

The Boyars of Romania associated the dragon with the "Devil"; Dracula is a diminutive, which means "the son of the devil". Vlad became the ruler of Wallachia in July of 1456. During his six-year reign, he committed many cruelties, and therefore established his controversial reputation.

Vlad Tepes adopted the method of impaling criminals and enemies and raising them aloft in the town square for all to see. Almost any crime, from lying and stealing to killing, could be punished by impalement. Being so confident in the effectiveness of his law, Vlad placed a golden cup on display in the central square of Tirgoviste.

The cup could be used by thirsty travellers, but had to remain on the square. According to the available historic sources, it was never stolen and remained unmolested throughout Vlad's reign. Crime and corruption ceased; commerce and culture thrived, and many Romanians to this day view Vlad Tepes as a hero for his fierce insistence on honesty and order.

The only real link between the historical Dracula and the modern literary myth of the vampire is the 1897 novel. Bram Stoker built his fictional character solely based on the research that he conducted in libraries in London. Political detractors and Saxon merchants, unhappy with the new trade regulations imposed by Vlad, did everything they could to blacken his reputation.

They produced and disseminated throughout Europe exaggerated stories and illustrations about Vlad's cruelty. Vlad Tepes' reign was however presented in a different way in chronicles written in other parts of Europe.

This evening was the captain's party where we queued up to be introduced to the captain, had a glass of sparkling wine and some polite conversation. At dinner we had the Parade of the Chefs, a tradition on most boats where the chefs march round with a tray of Baked Alaska, usually with sparklers – it is a way for the passengers to thank the unseen staff for their culinary efforts. Tonight, also, the Filipino staff on the ship provided us with a most entertaining show – these were all signs showing that the end of our trip was in sight.

Saturday 11ᵗʰ October

Nessebur Bulgaria

Overnight Sail to Nessebur, Bulgaria

Nessebur - Ship's Tender transfer to shore

Thishis was the first port in which we had to use the ship's tender. This took a little longer but was efficiently done and we were on the mainland in no time at all. Mainland may be the wrong term as Nessebur was once an island.

Nessebur - Transfer by Ship's Tender into the Harbour

Nessebur - The Isthmus access to the Mainland

Outlined against the sky, the ancient fortifications and venerable churches of the medieval town are a splendid sight. Nessebur has on several occasions found itself on the frontier of a threatened empire, and as such, it is a town with a rich history.

Nessebur - Heritage Site Access from the Isthmus thro' the ancient Fortifications

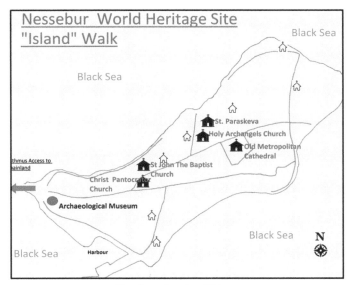

Nessebur – Location Map

The ancient part of the town is situated on a peninsula (previously an island) connected to the mainland by a narrow man-made isthmus, and it bears evidence of occupation by a variety of different civilisations over the course of its existence.

Its abundance of historic buildings prompted UNESCO to include Nessebur in its list of World Heritage Sites in 1983. You step through the gate, and jump back centuries.

Originally a small Thracian settlement of Mesembria, the town became a Greek colony when occupied by Dorians from Megara at the beginning of the 6th century BC. It turned into a thriving trading port and commercial centre from then on and a rival of Apollonia (Sozopol) across the water.

It remained the only Doric colony along the Black Sea coast as the rest were typically Ionic colonies. Remains from the Greek period include the Acropolis, a Temple of Apollo and an Agora.

A wall which formed part of the fortifications can still be seen on the north side of the peninsula. Bronze and silver coins were minted in the city from the 5th century BC and gold coins from the 3rd century BC.

The town fell under Roman rule in 71BC but it continued to enjoy privileges, such as the right to mint its own coinage. Not only beautiful but also hospitable, Nessebur has been attracting visitors for thousands of years.

Heredotus, the 5th century BC historian, was impressed by what he called " the city in the sea ", and four centuries later the geographer, Strabo, commented on how well the people got on with the neighbouring tribes.

Their friendly nature was an asset throughout their turbulent history. Repeatedly occupied by different powers of the region, the townsfolk always maintained their privileges by carefully cultivating good relations with their masters.

Mesembria was at its most prosperous when closely connected with Constantinople and it was one of the most important strongholds of the Byzantine Empire from the 5th century AD onwards. During this period many members of the imperial family and other nobles had villas on the island.

To show off their wealth, they built churches that are still the glory of Nessebur to this day. It became a Bishopric and four monumental Basilicas were built. The town was continually fought over by the Byzantines and Bulgar Turks, being captured and incorporated into the lands of the first Bulgarian Empire in 812 only to be ceded back to Byzantium a short time later and then re-conquered once more.

From the early 11th century, parts of Bulgaria shifted back and forward constantly between the two powers. In 1332 Nessebur, as it was now known, surrendered again to the Bulgarians under Tsar Ivan Alexander.

Trade and culture flourished and some of the most beautiful churches were built but disaster struck once more when the Crusaders, under Amadeus VI, Count of Savoy, conquered the town and handed it back to Byzantium.

Unfortunately, the great Byzantine Empire was about to be replaced by the Ottoman Turks who were massing around Constantinople. The capture of Nessebur by the Turks, marked the beginning of decline for the wealth of the citizens.

However, the people were permitted to remain Christians and keep their churches, although the town sank to a shadow of its former glorious self. It took 500 years for Nessebur, and Bulgaria to achieve their independence.

In 1877, Tsar Alexander II of Russia declared war on Turkey to free Bulgaria. In the aftermath of the Russo-Turkish wars, the Balkan wars and World War I, the country's borders shrank.

It was an ally of Germany in World War II and then fell under Soviet influence when it was invaded by the USSR, to become a People's Republic in 1946. Communist domination ended in 1990, when the country held its first multi-party election and began moving towards democracy.

In 2001, Simeon Borisov Saxe-Coburg, the former King who was forced from his throne after WW II, returned to power as prime minister. It joined the EU in 2007.

Around the end of the 19th century, Nessebur was merely a fishermen's and vinegrower's village but it has seen much development in the 20th Century with a new town being built and the ancient one being restored.

In 1956, the town was proclaimed an Architectural and Archaeological Reserve and as soon as we set foot through the west gate we found traces of the fortifying wall dating from the 6th century BC and the long defensive harbour wall put up three centuries later, which was discovered under water.

However the remains of the early Byzantine buildings are the best preserved in this Archaeological Museum, as this whole 25 hectare area is known.

Once the town boasted 40 places of worship clustered in this confined space, although only ten have survived, all masterpieces of Byzantine and early Balkan religious architecture.

Whether built during the Byzantine, Bulgarian or Ottoman rule of the city, the Churches of Nessebur represent the rich architectural heritage of the Eastern Orthodox world and illustrate the gradual development from Early Christian Basilicas to medieval cross-domed Churches.

The Main Street led us to the 14th century Church of Christ Pantocrator with its little garden.

Nessebur - Church of Christ Pantocrator (Ruler Of The Universe)

The three-lobed nave and most of the towers are still intact and are enhanced by the arcades and rich celadon ceramic inlays that typify late-Byzantine architecture.

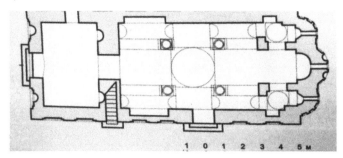

A Cruciform dome church with 3 altar niches, a natherex and a bell tower above the natherex. Pillars support the dome. Inside the apses are semi-circular and outside five walled, built in the first half of the 14th Century. Everyone noticed the line of swastika shapes set into the brickwork all round the building. Of course, this symbol did not hold the significance it has for our generation today, but was merely a primitive religious ornament in the shape of a Greek cross.

Nessebur - External views of the Church of Christ Pantocrator

Nessebur - 11th Century St John the Baptist Church

Just to the north was the 11th century St John the Baptist Church which we were told has a fresco of Saint Marina pulling a devil from the sea, ready to beat its head with a hammer.

The 13th century donor, in exchange for his largesse, is painted radiating goodness and spirituality. Unfortunately, the building was not open and we could only imagine the scene.

The Church of the Holy Archangels, with its lovely ceramic decorations and brick chequerboard vaults and niches, stands on picturesque Alehoi Street, overhung with wooden houses carved with fish and sun symbols.

Nessebur - Church of the Holy Archangels

Nessebur - Ceramic decoration details

Nessebur - Overhung houses – Alehoi Street

Scattered around the old town are these distinctive Messambrian houses, constructed in the 19th century in the Eastern Rumelian style typical for the Bulgarian Black Sea coast.

Nessebur - Additional views – Overhung houses – Alehoi Street

Normally they have an austere grey-stone ground floor with a jutting, wooden upper storey with overhanging eaves and large oriel windows, which let in floods of light. Inside, all the wooden doors, ceilings and cupboards have been artistically carved.

A few steps along the old cobbled streets was St. Paraskeva still displaying its green ceramic ornamentation, despite the church's state of ruin.

Nessebur – St Paraskeva Church

Nessebur - Church of the Holy Saviour - St Spas

Nessebur - The Old Metropolitan Cathedral

Down in the main square, now beginning to be thronged with souvenir sellers, - I can't imagine what it is like in the summer season - stands one of the most important monuments, the Old Metropolitan Cathedral, founded in the 6th century and rebuilt in the 9th.

It was here that the bishops officiated in the town's more prosperous days. Being the oldest church in town, it is thought to stand over the ancient agora or public meeting place.

In the 15th century power passed from the Old to the New Metropolitan Cathedral (11th century), also called St. Stephen's. The most beautiful of Nessebur's churches, a masterpiece of Byzantine religious architecture, it is decorated with superb 16th century murals.

The patron who financed the enlargement of the church in the 15th century stands piously among the west wall's "Forty Martyrs". Opposite, are the hastily restored ruins of St. John Aliturgetos, built of white limestone slabs and red brick, looking out over the sea.

Nessebur - St John Aliturgetos

It is said that the church was never consecrated and put to use as a house of worship because it was too sumptuous – something difficult to imagine in its present condition. Our guide now said we had some free time until we left for lunch.

Nessebur - A Local musical instrument shop – Above and Below

We wandered round the streets looking at the various little shops –
one was a most colourful and unusual music shop - then we had a cool
drink at the point of the island overlooking the sea including our ship

anchored offshore and then finally wandered down to the picturesque little harbour where the fishermen were mending their nets.

A View of the Nessebur Harbour area

Nessebur - Local fishing boats

M V Discovery at anchor

Leaving the coast and this legacy of a chequered past, we headed inland to the heart of the Bulgarian countryside and the village of Bata. The countryside, away from the sea and the modern resorts, was very barren and only had small enclaves of cottages and individual patches of garden in which to grow vegetables for each family's personal use.

Nessebur - Local Transport

A smattering of wood carving and pottery stalls were also set up by the roadside to attract the tourists. We arrived at a walled garden, where an enterprising family had built a large area for tables and entertainment in the open air. Fortunately, the weather was dry and sunny.

Bata - Lunch Venue - Offering on entry

Lunch Table Service

As we entered we were offered a large loaf from which we had to pluck out a morsel. This is an old symbol of kind hospitality but after seeing a hundred unwashed hands diving into the bread, I quietly disposed of my piece and advised Graham to do the same. The food was reasonable, but I had my doubts about the kitchen which seemed to be about four feet squared – it reminded me of the huge Majorcan barbecues which were prevalent in the 1960's and 1970's. We drank plenty of wine and raki and we did not end up with stomach problems so my fears were ungrounded.

Local dancing entertainment – Above and Below

Local dancing and costumes

Our entertainment by the young dancers was both colourful and enjoyable and on leaving we watched some athletic fire- walking on a pit in the garden, where they also had pottery and wood carving workshops. It had been a pleasant and relaxing afternoon and the people were warm and friendly.

Bare feet fire-walking demonstration

On returning to the coast, we found a huge queue of passengers waiting for the ship's tender. Apparently, the sea had developed quite a swell and the tenders were having difficulty.

Ship's tender transfers

Half an hour later, we were on our way but after trying to dock three times, unsuccessfully, the tender pilot decided to go round to the other side of the ship.

Tender transfer - Sea legs definitely required

Here they had lowered a sort of rope ladder and after much to-ing and fro-ing, each of us was pushed onto the ladder.

It was a strenuous climb especially with the sea splashing in my face but I made it and so did Graham – just another little bit of excitement!

Tonight, on board, the theme was French (don't ask me why) with a French meal and show "Bonjour Paris".

I will mention just a couple of little bits of additional information before we leave Bulgaria. This country is one of the world's biggest producers of rose oil – it was for sale in all the shops.

The reason for this is hidden in the high quality of the Bulgarian Kazanluk rose (Kazanlashkaroza), a special type that was cultivated after many years of production and development. The Bulgarian roses are inheritors of the Damascena oil-bearing rose which was brought there a long time ago and has been cultivated in the Rose Valley for more than 300 years.

The rose oil is referred to as "liquid gold" as it is a very expensive product, used mainly for the making of perfumes, chocolates, liqueurs and jam. One kilogram of rose oil can be extracted from 3,000 kg of roses, which means that for one gram of rose oil, more than 1,300 rose blossoms are used.

Every flower is picked by hand and preserved carefully for distillation and more than 2,000 people are occupied in the harvest every year as the period for the harvest lasts only 20-25 days.

The distillation method is the same as for raki (a type of digestive brandy) and the rose oil was discovered accidentally when they were trying to improve the production of rose water.

Returning to Greek mythology once more – Orpheus, the great musician of Greek myth, whose songs could charm wild beasts and coax even rocks to move, was said to have been born in the ancient land of Bulgaria.

Finally, a must in Bulgaria, is the thick, creamy yoghurt. After all, the Bulgarians did invent it, as its Latin name testifies, Lactobacillus bulgaricus.

Setting sail from Bulgaria

Sunday 12th October

Istanbul, Turkey

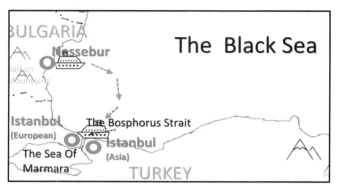

Overnight sailing to Istanbul

We awoke once more to one of the loveliest skylines in the world. Curving domes, rising in layers, with minarets soaring upward, all wrapped in a gauzy blue veil.

This old city of Istanbul is literally, where east meets west with a foot on two continents, Europe and Asia, separated by the Bosphorus. It looks oriental, but for a thousand years it was the intellectual centre of the Western World. Over the centuries it has had four names:

- Byzantium to the Greeks when it was founded in the 7th century BC,
- Nova Roma or New Rome when the Emperor Constantine transferred the capital of the Roman world here, then
- Constantinople in his honour, and, finally
- Istanbul from the Greek "eis ten polin", i.e. "to the city".

Like Rome, it is built on seven hills and joined by old and new bridges, for Istanbul is not just east and west but old and new, a city of a thousand moods and faces.

Places Visited in Istanbul

Black Sea →

Bosphorus Bridge

Istanbul - European Side (Aurupa Yaksai)

Beylerbeyi Palace

Golden Horn

The Bosphorus

District Of Uskudar (Scutari)

Leander's Tower

Salacak

Istanbul - Asian Side (Anadolu Yakasi)

Mosque Of The Grand Visier Rustem Pasa

Spice Bazaar (Misis Carsisi)

Suleymaniye Mosque

(Old Istanbul)

N

Haghia Sophia

(Selimiye Barracks)

To Ankara

To The Aegean Sea

British Cemetery

Sea of Marmara

M V Discovery (On the left) berthed on the Bosphorus on the European side of Istanbul

As we had been in Istanbul earlier in the year, we decided to visit parts which we had missed on our first visit. This meant crossing the Bosphorus to the Asian side.

From the Ship's berth, crossing the Bosphorus Bridge to the Asian side

We stopped at Salacak to admire the marvellous views of the city and watch the morning ferries on the Bosphorus plying their trade and taking passengers to their work or, as it was Sunday, perhaps to visit relatives.

Salacak's view across the Bosphorus - Sultanahmet Mosque to the left and the Topkapi Palace to the right

Leander's Tower was right in front of us here. I have already described this in detail in another travelogue but I will give a brief summary. Located on a small island off the shore of the peaceful district of Uskudar, the tiny white tower is a well-known landmark, dating from the 18th century. The tower, surrounded by various myths, once served as a quarantine centre during a cholera outbreak, as a lighthouse, a custom's control point and a maritime toll gate.

Leander's Tower

It was refurbished in 1999 and is now a very pricey restaurant and disco.

We drove on into the district of Uskudar, which enjoys an intriguing coexistence between Islamic traditionalists and a growing colony of avant-garde artists and writers. After the bustle of European Istanbul, it is a pleasure to wander around this district with not another tourist in sight.

Selimiye Barracks (Scutari) — Where Florence Nightingale and her nurses worked during the Crimean War

Climbing the hill, we passed the Selimiye Barracks. These were originally made of wood and completed in 1799 under the Sultan Selim III. They were built to house the "New Army" that formed part of his plan to reform the Imperial command structure and replace the powerful Janissaries. The plan backfired and Selim was deposed but the barracks were, nevertheless, a striking symbol of Constantinople's military might, becoming more so when they were built in stone in 1829 by Mahmut II.

The building still houses Istanbul's First Army Division and is off limits to the public. Of course, in the 19th century, Europeans called this area Scutari and it served as a British military base in the Crimean War. The British nurse, Florence Nightingale (1820-1910) was a tireless campaigner for hospital, military and social reform.

During the Crimean War, she organized a party of 38 nurses to take charge of the medical services at the Selimiye barracks. She was appalled at the conditions that the wounded and sick soldiers were enduring at the hands of the military.

The majority were dying of cholera and infected wounds and by the time she returned to Britain in 1856, at the end of the war, the mortality rate in the barracks had decreased from 20 to 2 percent, and the fundamental principles of modern nursing had been established.

Although the barracks are off limits, visits can be made on application to army headquarters and there is a small museum containing some original furniture and the famous lamp which gave her the epitaph of "Lady of the Lamp".

British Cemetery Monument - Crimean War   *British Cemetery War Memorial*

Nearby, after walking past the military guard, we arrived at the British Cemetery, the final resting place of almost 6,000 soldiers, many of whom lost their lives to cholera during the Crimean War.

It was a quiet peaceful park, high on a hill, overlooking the Bosphorus. As we walked around the graveyard reading the various epitaphs, we discovered, sadly, that a large number of Scottish soldiers were lying here along with a huge group of young Scottish doctors, all having died of cholera.

It was discovered not long ago, during some archaeological digging, that the barracks where the hospital had been constructed, lay directly over an open sewer – what chance did they have!

This view from a Beylerbeyi Palace window shows The Bosphorus Frontage

The only palace built by the Ottomans on the Asian side of the Bosphorus, is the Beylerbeyi Palace. Designed in the Baroque style of the late Ottoman period, Beylerbeyi was built between 1861 and 1865 by members of the Balyan family under the orders of the Sultan Abdul Aziz.

An earlier palace of timber had occupied the site and the terraced gardens were already laid out by Murat IV in 1639.

The Beylerbeyi Palace – front facade

As the Ottoman empire withered, palaces proliferated in a flourish of grandeur and showmanship.

Abdul Aziz had Beylerbeyi built as a summer and pleasure palace to entertain dignitaries and royalty.

This fantasy in white marble has two sections, Selamlik (men) and Harem (women), arranged on two floors, with two splendid marble staircases giving access to each section independently. The palace contains 6 halls and 24 rooms.

The Beylerbeyi Palace - front façade

The Beylerbeyi Palace - Double marble main staircase

The most attractive room is the reception hall, on the ground floor, which has a pool and fountain. Running water was always popular in Ottoman houses for its pleasant sound and cooling effect.

The Beylerbeyi Palace - Reception Hall

This room along with the Blue room on the first floor and the flanking chambers constitute the men's quarters. The Harem hall and rooms are smaller in scale. Since this was a summer palace there is no central heating system nor are there any chimneys. Many rooms have marquetry panelling and the columns are stuccoed and painted to resemble marble. The ceilings are decorated with geometrical patterns and colourful floral bouquets.

The Beylerbeyi Palace - Mirror reflections and Bohemian crystal chandeliers

Ceiling Naval Painting

Amidst these are frescoes of Ottoman warships. The patron of the palace, Abdul Aziz, was a patron of the navy. Under his guidance, the Ottoman fleet became second only to the British fleet and this accounts for the various paintings of ships on the ceiling. It appears that the Sultan, also a keen painter, drew sketches for the ceiling decorations himself. Much of the furniture in the palace is European with gilded suites of chairs amidst gilded cornices, mirrors and consoles, all French in origin. The curtains and upholstery materials, all original, are Hereke silks and most of the rugs are from a similar source.

European style furnishings

Crystal chandeliers from Bohemia are suspended from the ceilings of many rooms and they give the palace an entirely different character. Vases of the Far East, China, Japan and European Sèvres can be seen standing alongside Yildiz ware from the porcelain factory founded in the reign of Abdulhamit. Many of the clocks are French with one most notable timepiece being a table clock in the Blue room, a boulle silver clock weighing 60 kgs.

There are now three bathrooms in the palace although when it was built there was only one, which was contained in the imperial suite of the Sultan. Two later additions were from the period of Abdulhamit.

The Empress Eugenie of France, the wife of Napoleon III, was a guest at the palace in 1869 on her way to the opening of the Suez Canal. She stayed in the imperial suite and it was rumoured that there was a romantic affair between the Sultan and the lady. The Duke and Duchess of Windsor were also guests of the palace. The longest resident in the palace was the hapless and autocratic Abdulhamit II. Third –but last of the line of sultans, he was brought back from exile in Thessalonica to spend six years as a prisoner here. After being deposed in 1909, he died in Beylerbeyi, virtually forgotten. To keep himself distracted Abdul Aziz also had a zoo built on the site and, apparently, delighted in the flocks of ostriches and several Bengal tigers.

Examples of the furniture made by Sultan Abdulhamit II
who was an accomplished cabinetmaker

The terraced grounds once covered an area of 160,000square metres and as well as the zoo, contained hunting grounds, conservatories and formal gardens of note with plants and trees from all over the world. The zoo is no longer there and the gardens have been reduced by half because the land was required for roads and schools.

The jetty of Beylerbeyi is embellished with two shore pavilions for bathing – one for the Harem and the other for the Selamlik (the men's quarters). The whole visit to this palace was for us, alone, and it was very exciting walking around on the sumptuous carpets and sitting on grandiose furniture especially in parts formerly forbidden to women. It was as if we had crept in secretly and nobody knew we were there. I don't know what the Sultan would have thought.

Gate to the Bosphorus Jetty – Accessed from the Beylerbeyi Palace front garden

Beylerbeyi Palace Jetty Gate and the adjoining First Bosphorus Bridge

The First Bosphorus Suspension Bridge – Looking towards the European part

The Suleymaniye Mosque

*Mosque of Grand Vizier
Rustem Pasa*

We now returned to the bustle of the city where had lunch in a
restaurant near Haghia Sophia, not quite as nice as our restaurants
earlier in the year, but perfectly adequate. I was amazed when the
dessert came and it was baklava, my favourite, and that most of our
fellow travellers had not come across this dish, and left it uneaten

because of the green filling of pistachios – everyone to their own, but they missed a treat.

This afternoon, our itinerary stated that we were to visit the huge Suleymaniye Mosque, the main landmark of Istanbul, but I knew this would not be possible as it had been, and still was, undergoing massive refurbishment.

Raised above the shops and warehouses of the city's Spice Bazaar is one of Sinan, the architect's, finest works - the mosque of Grand Vizier Rustem Pasa, son-in-law of Suleyman I and this was our destination .

Although there is no inscription giving the construction date of the mosque, a foundation document indicates that it was built in around 1561.

The architect, concerned that the mosque should not be lost among the market buildings, raised it up on deep vaults in a most innovative way. Consequently there is no large court fronting the mosque and the only way to reach the entrance is up a series of very old flights of steps.

The Mosque of Grand Vizier Rustem Pasa – Central Dome

The central section of the mosque is surmounted by a large dome flanked by four semi-domes and supported by 8 piers – the minaret was destroyed in 1964.

The staggering wealth of the decoration says something about the amount of money that the corrupt Rustem managed to salt away – he was later disgraced.

The Mosque of Grand Vizier Rustem Pasa – Prayer Hall

The Mosque of Grand Vizier Rustem Pasa – Tile decoration

Most of the interior is covered in Iznik tiles of the highest quality. The 4 piers are adorned with tiles of one design, but the rest of the prayer hall is a riot of different patterns, from abstract to florals. Some of the finest tiles can be found in the galleries, making it the most magnificently tiled mosque in the city. On return to the ship, we then had to face the onerous task of packing as we were travelling no further on the ship.

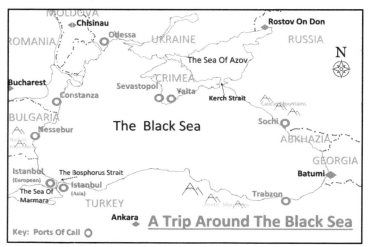

In the evening, we had arranged to join the couple from our table for an oriental dinner in the Yacht Club and the show afterwards – a fitting end to a most enjoyable and informative trip.

On Monday the 13th October, we endured the endless waiting around and the tedious flights back home, once more.

---oOo---

NOTES

Note (1).
Additional Day In Sochi instead of Batumi, Georgia

An unstable situation had arisen in this area because of the Russian fleet patrolling the Black Sea near the annexed port of Poti, which was not far from the Georgia City of Batumi, originally one of our ports of call.

Accordingly it had been necessary in the cruise itinerary to add an additional day at Sochi, Russia, instead of berthing at Batumi.

Note (2).
Georgia / Russia - Abkhazia

Abkhazia is situated in the north-western corner of Georgia with the Black Sea to the south-west and the Caucasus mountains to the north-east .

In 1992 -93 this region fought and won a war of secession with Georgia and declared its independence in 1999 maintaining an ever closer partnership with Russia. See location on the Black Sea Map.

Note (3).
Ukraine / Russia - Crimea - Yalta and Sevastopol

The Crimean Peninsula, located in the north of the Black Sea, was annexed by the Russian Federation in 2014 and since then has been administered as two Russian federal subjects - the Republic of Crimea and the Federal City of Sevastopol.

The annexation from Ukraine followed a Russian military intervention in the Crimean Peninsula in the aftermath of the 2014 Ukrainian revolution. Sevastopol, located in Crimea then became a strategic and permanent warm water port for the Russian Black Sea Fleet.

As a consequence the Russian control of the cities of Yalta and Sevastopol no longer accommodates the free access by tourists as was the earlier situation in 2008 when Audrey travelled there.

Note (4).
Odessa – Alexander Pushkin Museum

Pushkin House in Odessa, later to become the Alexander Pushkin Museum, has always been popular with local people and it became a symbol of their home for the defenders during the war in Odessa in 1941.

It was a great shock for everyone in Odessa when part of the building was destroyed in the German bombardment on the city however after the end of the war this building was one of the first to be restored.

-ooOoo-

List Of Individual Maps

(1) Numeral Refers To Notes

ACKNOWLEDGEMENTS

- Posthumously To Audrey - Mine has been an entirely support role in adding the presentation aspects and photographs to the complete text manuscript that she had completed.

I know that she was methodical in checking all her facts and completed that to the very best of her ability. In acquiring these facts I know that she endeavoured not to infringe any copyright issues.

This was a task completed by her primarily to generate a library of books, of which this is one, in the knowledge that the travel experiences and locations she had had the good fortune to visit and which, in the fullness of time may not all survive as she had known them, but that her books would provide a descriptive and pictorial record that our grandchildren, when older, could read and enjoy.

It also provides a similar opportunity for adults with a curiosity surrounding travel to enjoy as well.

Accordingly it would be remiss of me, as her husband, and having seen at first hand the enormous effort it took for her to complete these texts at a time when her health was sadly deteriorating, not to acknowledge her sacrifice and ultimate achievement. She was a fighter as well as having a talented mind.

-To Kim and Sinclair Macleod from Indie Authors World, indieauthorsworld.com, for their constructive and supportive comments and helpful advice to me in putting these texts into book form.

- To our 6 grandchildren and 2 Bumps that Audrey knew but which I have come to know as 8 young individual and curious persons whom I love so much.

- To the people of the countries we visited – to thank them for their kind hospitality and friendship.

This is the second volume in a 'Tales Of A Grandmother' Book Series which are the produce of the late Audrey Forsyth.

In these she shares and brings to life her travel experiences and love of language, culture, history, music and people.

Audrey's Tales are all the more moving when one considers that this and the many other manuscripts in her **Tales Of A Grandmother** Series were completed by her, but not published, in her lifetime.

A 25% share of book proceeds is donated to the charity Pancreatic Cancer Uk to help fund life-saving research.

pancreaticcanceruk.org.uk

For Readers' Information

'The Wonders Of Nepal' is Audrey's first book published in her 'Tales Of A Grandmother' Series and is available from Amazon.

Not To Be Missed

Further volumes, in preparation, and to follow on are...
The Wonders of South America
The Wonders of Russia
The Wonders of Turkey
All are interesting, diverse, enlightening and unique -
Further Up-to-date information is available
on the Tales Of A Grandmother Website
talesofagrandmother.com
Enjoy!

*Travel makes one modest. You see what a tiny place
you occupy in the world" -* **Gustave Flaubert**

Lightning Source UK Ltd.
Milton Keynes UK
UKHW051642090122
396726UK00010B/190